D1123526

Modern Middle East Nations
AND THEIR STRATEGIC PLACE IN THE WORLD

SUDAN

Modern Middle East Nations
AND THEIR STRATEGIC PLACE IN THE WORLD

SUDAN

GAIL SNYDER

MASON CREST PUBLISHERS
PHILADELPHIA

Produced by OTTN Publishing, Stockton, New Jersey

Mason Crest Publishers
370 Reed Road
Broomall, PA 19008
www.masoncrest.com

First printing

1 3 5 7 9 8 6 4 2

Library of Congress Cataloging-in-Publication Data

Snyder, Gail.
  Sudan / Gail Snyder.
    p. cm. — (Modern Middle East nations and their strategic place
in the world)
Summary: Discusses the geography, history, economy, government,
religion, people, foreign relations, and major cities of Sudan.
Includes bibliographical references and index.
  ISBN 1-59084-519-6
1. Sudan—Juvenile literature.   [1. Sudan.]   I. Title. II. Series.
DT154.6.S69 2003
962.4—dc21
                                              2002013011

Modern Middle East Nations
AND THEIR STRATEGIC PLACE IN THE WORLD

TABLE OF CONTENTS

Modern Middle East Nations
AND THEIR STRATEGIC PLACE IN THE WORLD

Dr. Harvey Sicherman, president and director of the Foreign Policy Research Institute, is the author of such books as *America the Vulnerable: Our Military Problems and How to Fix Them* (2002) and *Palestinian Autonomy, Self-Government and Peace* (1993).

Introduction

by Dr. Harvey Sicherman

Situated as it is between Africa, Europe, and the Far East, the Middle East has played a unique role in world history. Often described as the birthplace of religions (notably Judaism, Christianity, and Islam) and the cradle of civilizations (Egypt, Mesopotamia, Persia), this region and its peoples have given humanity some of its most precious possessions. At the same time, the Middle East has had more than its share of conflicts. The area is strewn with the ruins of fortifications and the cemeteries of combatants, not to speak of modern arsenals for war.

Today, more than ever, Americans are aware that events in the Middle East can affect our security and prosperity. The United States has a considerable military, political, and economic presence throughout much of the region. Developments there regularly find their way onto the front pages of our newspapers and the screens of our television sets.

Still, it is fair to say that most Middle Eastern countries remain a mystery, their cultures and religions barely known, their peoples and politics confusing and strange. The purpose of this book series is to change that, to educate the reader in the basic facts about the 23 states and many peoples that make up the region. (For our purpose, the Middle East also includes the North African states linked by ethnicity, language, and religion to the Arabs, as well as Somalia and Mauritania, which are African but share the Muslim religion and are members of the Arab League.) A notable feature of the series is the integration of geography, demography, and history; economics and politics; culture and religion. The careful student will learn much that he or she needs to know about ever so important lands.

A few general observations are in order as an introduction to the subject matter.

The first has to do with history and politics. The modern Middle East is full of ancient sites and peoples who trace their lineage and literature to antiquity. Many commentators also attribute the Middle East's political conflicts to grievances and rivalries from the distant past. While history is often invoked, the truth is that the modern Middle East political system dates only from the 1920s and was largely created by the British and the French, the victors of World War I. Such states as Algeria, Iraq, Israel, Jordan, Kuwait, Saudi Arabia, Syria, Turkey, and the United Arab Emirates did not exist before 1914—they became independent between 1920 and 1971. Others, such as Egypt and Iran, were dominated by outside powers until well after World War II. Before 1914, most of the region's states were either controlled by the Turkish-run Ottoman Empire or owed allegiance to the Ottoman sultan. (The sultan was also the caliph or highest religious authority in Islam, in the line of the prophet Muhammad's successors, according to the beliefs of the majority of Muslims known as the Sunni.) It was this imperial Muslim system that was ended by the largely British military victory over the Ottomans in World War I. Few of the leaders who emerged in the wake of this event were happy with the territories they were assigned or the borders, which were often drawn by Europeans. Yet, the system has endured despite many efforts to change it.

The second observation has to do with economics, demography, and natural resources. The Middle Eastern peoples live in a region of often dramatic geographical contrasts: vast parched deserts and high mountains, some with year-round snow; stone-hard volcanic rifts and lush semi-tropical valleys; extremely dry and extremely wet conditions, sometimes separated by only a few miles; large permanent rivers and *wadis*, riverbeds dry as a bone until winter rains send torrents of flood from the mountains to the sea. In ancient times, a very skilled agriculture made the Middle East the breadbasket of the Roman Empire, and its trade carried luxury fabrics, foods, and spices both East and West.

Most recently, however, the Middle East has become more known for a single commodity—oil, which is unevenly distributed and largely concentrated in the Persian Gulf and Arabian Peninsula (although large pockets are also to be found in Algeria, Libya, and other sites). There are also new, potentially lucrative offshore gas fields in the Eastern Mediterranean.

This uneven distribution of wealth has been compounded by demographics. Birth rates are very high, but the countries with the most oil are often lightly populated. Over the last decade, Middle East populations under the age of 20 have grown enormously. How will these young people be educated? Where will they work? The failure of most governments in the region to give their people skills and jobs (with notable exceptions such as Israel) has also contributed to large out-migrations. Many have gone to Europe; many others work in other Middle Eastern countries, supporting their families from afar.

Another unsettling situation is the heavy pressure both people and industry have put on vital resources. Chronic water shortages plague the region. Air quality, public sanitation, and health services in the big cities are also seriously overburdened. There are solutions to these problems, but they require a cooperative approach that is sorely lacking.

A third important observation is the role of religion in the Middle East. Americans, who take separation of church and state for granted, should know that most countries in the region either proclaim their countries to be Muslim or allow a very large role for that religion in public life. Among those with predominantly Muslim populations, Turkey alone describes itself as secular and prohibits avowedly religious parties in the political system. Lebanon was a Christian-dominated state, and Israel continues to be a Jewish state. While both strongly emphasize secular politics, religion plays an enormous role in culture, daily life, and legislation. It is also important to recall that Islamic law (*Sharia*) permits people to practice Judaism and Christianity in Muslim states but only as *Dhimmi*, protected but very second-class citizens.

Fourth, the American student of the modern Middle East will be impressed by the varieties of one-man, centralized rule, very unlike the workings of Western democracies. There are monarchies, some with traditional methods of consultation for tribal elders and even ordinary citizens, in Saudi Arabia and many Gulf States; kings with limited but still important parliaments (such as in Jordan and

INTRODUCTION

Morocco); and military and civilian dictatorships, some (such as Syria) even operating on the hereditary principle (Hafez al Assad's son Bashar succeeded him). Turkey is a practicing democracy, although a special role is given to the military that limits what any government can do. Israel operates the freest democracy, albeit constricted by emergency regulations (such as military censorship) due to the Arab-Israeli conflict.

In conclusion, the MODERN MIDDLE EAST NATIONS series will engage imagination and interest simply because it covers an area of such great importance to the United States. Americans may be relative latecomers to the affairs of this region, but our involvement there will endure. We at the Foreign Policy Research Institute hope that these books will kindle a lifelong interest in the fascinating and significant Middle East.

This photograph, which won the Pulitzer Prize in 1994, captures the view many people in the West have of Sudan: despair and death. Since becoming an independent country in the 1950s, Sudan has been devastated by a brutal civil war that has killed millions of people and forced millions more to flee their homes.

Place in the World

A little girl, weak and desperate for nourishment, tries to reach some food while a vulture patiently waits for her to die. That is the image many people hold of Sudan: desperate poverty, famine, and strife from decades of civil war.

That civil war, which began shortly after the country declared its independence from British and Egyptian rule in 1956, has claimed the lives of more than two million Sudanese. The fighting between the Arab Islamic north, headquartered in the country's capital in Khartoum, and the largely black African nomadic tribes in the south, has killed more people than the combined casualties from fighting in Rwanda, Somalia, Angola, Bosnia, Chechnya, Kosovo, Liberia, Sierra Leone, and the 1991 Persian Gulf War. In a country that is home to more than 37 million residents—and in total area is the largest country in Africa (approximately the size of the continental United States east of the

Osama bin Laden planned the August 1998 attacks on the American embassies in Tanzania and Kenya, the October 2000 bombing of the USS *Cole* in Yemen, and the September 11, 2001, attack on the World Trade Center in New York City and the Pentagon in Washington D.C. Bin Laden directed his terrorist al-Qaeda network from Sudan between 1991 and 1996.

Mississippi River)—at least 4 million Sudanese have been forced to leave their homes because of the fighting.

Surprisingly, the war in Sudan and its massive human toll has attracted little sympathy from countries around the world. Stung by the Sudan government's support of Iraq in the 1991 Gulf War, and angered during the 1990s when Sudan harbored the terrorist leader Osama bin Laden (mastermind of the September 11, 2001, terrorist attacks on the World Trade Center in New York and Pentagon in Washington, D.C.), the United States has limited its role in the Sudanese conflict to supplying **humanitarian aid** to the starving and displaced people. In 1998, shortly after followers of bin Laden bombed two American embassies in Africa, President Bill Clinton ordered a cruise missile strike on a pharmaceutical factory near Khartoum, alleging that the plant manufactured chemical weapons (this was later found to be untrue). American intelligence agencies also believed that bin Laden had established at least three terrorist training camps in Sudan.

Although the decades of fighting in Sudan have occasionally been interrupted by lengthy cease-fires, neither side has been able to make measurable progress toward peace. In fact, the recent discovery of oil in the southern part of the country has made matters worse. This valuable commodity, now bringing the government revenues of more than $500 million a year, is helping to pay for the war and giving the government new reasons to drive the *indigenous* people away from the oil rich lands.

In 2001, the United Nations placed Sudan near the bottom of its list of countries rated by their degree of human development. Sudan came in at number 138 out of 162 countries compared by life expectancy, educational attainment, and income. No doubt this ranking would not have surprised British General Charles Gordon, who wrote more than 120 years ago:

> The Sudan is a useless possession, ever was so, and ever will be so. . . . No one who has ever lived in the Sudan can escape the reflection, "What a useless possession is this land." Few men can stand its fearful monotony and deadly climate.

Yet the fact that so many are willing to fight over this grim country suggests it is a valuable land. Five hundred different peoples live there and they speak in a hundred languages. Sudan's native people are known for their kindness and willingness to share whatever small portions of food they have. At the same time, it is one of the few places left on Earth where slavery is still practiced, ritual circumcision of young girls is common, and where ancient punishments such as stonings and amputations are meted out as justice.

The Nile River, the world's longest river, flows through the Nubian desert of northern Sudan, near Wadi Halfa. The river's name comes from the Greek word *neilos*, which means "river valley."

The Land

Sudan is unique in the enormous differences in climate and landforms that occur within its borders. The Arabic name for the country is Bilad al-Sudan, which means "land of the blacks." The country covers nearly a million square miles of desert, **savanna**, rainforest, and swamp. In area, it is the largest country in Africa and ninth largest in the world.

The heat in Sudan can be oppressive. Sudan is located north of the Equator, in a region known as the Torrid Zone. This area is between two lines of latitude above and below the Equator (the Tropic of Cancer in the northern hemisphere and the Tropic of Capricorn in the southern hemisphere). The Torrid Zone receives more direct sunlight than any other part of the earth.

Land in Sudan is mostly flat plain with the exception of several mountain ranges. The Red Sea Hills overlook the Red Sea in the east. Another range of hills is the Marra Mountains

(Jebal Marrah), located in the western portion of the country near Chad. In the south, near Kenya, visitors can find the Didinga Hills, Dongotona Mountains, and the Imatong Mountains. Centrally located in Sudan are the Nuba Mountains, where before the civil war people grew **sorghum** and cotton in the rich soil.

THE IMPORTANCE OF THE NILE

"You create the grain, you bring forth the barley, assuring perpetuity to the temples. If you cease your toil and your work, then all that exists is in anguish," says a hymn to the Nile written more than 4,000 years ago. Today, the Nile remains the lifeblood of Sudan and its people. The world's longest river, the Nile runs some 3,470 miles from Tanzania in Central Africa to Egypt in North Africa, passing through Sudan on its way to the Mediterranean Sea.

As the river meanders through Sudan, it travels through territory that remains wild and untamed. A steamer trip on the Nile might take as much as eight days to travel the length of the country, some 1,200 miles (1,900 km). Along the way, a visitor will see elephants, lions, cheetahs, zebras, giraffes, and other animals. All manner of tropical insects and spiders inhabit the banks. Tsetse flies and mosquitoes can spread the disease malaria.

As the Nile flows through the Eastern part of the country from south to north, it provides drinking water for people and animals, a home for fish, a source of electricity, and—when its annual summer flood arrives—rich sediment for growing crops. Rainfall dramatically increases in the summer when moisture-laden winds blow in from the Congo River Basin. Drought and famine will occur if these winds are late in developing, as they often were during the 1970s and 1980s.

The Nile River is actually two rivers: the Blue Nile, which flows across Sudan from Ethiopia; and the White Nile, which enters Sudan from Uganda. The White Nile is the longer and calmer of the

Geographic features of Sudan, the largest country in Africa, include the Nile River valley, and several mountain ranges. The Sudd, an enormous area of swamp and wetlands, is located south of the Nuba Mountains.

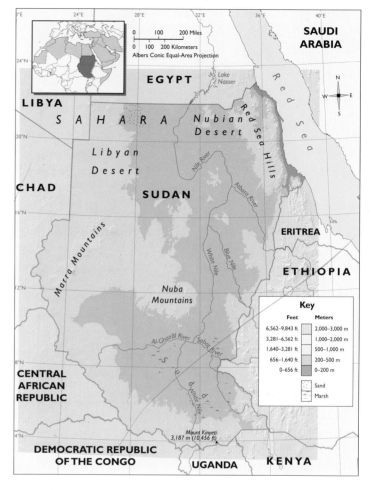

two, but the Blue Nile provides most of the water when the two rivers finally join as one. The two Niles are named for the color of their water. While water in the White Nile appears more muddy gray than white, if one stands at the Blue Nile at dawn or dusk its water will be very blue.

The Blue Nile first makes its appearance in Sudan in the sparse village of Bumbodi, where simple huts dot the riverbank's scrubby landscape. It then passes through Fazughli, known for its gold mines, and Roseieres. Here, the river flows through a rocky waterfall called a **cataract**, one of six that occur in the river that make navigation difficult.

Leaving Roseieres, the river rolls past vast plains broken now and then by large hills known as *jebels*. As it flows past the town of Sennar, the Blue Nile gets wider, slower and warmer. Above Sennar, desert sands practically touch the river; not much grows there

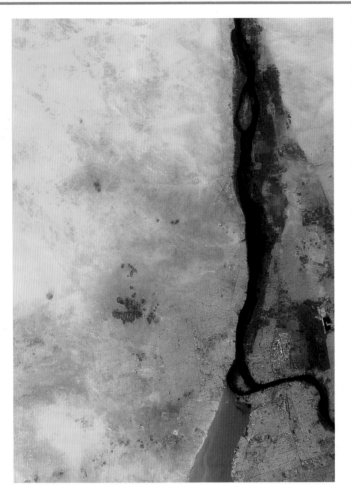

This image, taken by a NASA satellite on August 30, 2001, shows Sudan's capital, Khartoum, and flooded farmland along the Nile River. Khartoum can be seen at the lower right, at the confluence of the White (left) and Blue (right) Nile Rivers. Flooded farmland along the banks of the Nile appears dark blue. The surrounding desert is colored pink.

In recent years Nile flooding has been a major problem. The 2001 flood was the highest in 20 years; it inundated about 70,000 acres of farmland and displaced some 7,000 families from their homes. As a result of the flooding, Sudan's grain harvest was reduced. This added to the shortages of food already existing in the country.

without irrigation. Two tributaries called the Dinder and the Rahad meet the Blue Nile, adding their power to the river as it flows north to Khartoum, the capital of Sudan, where it will come together with the White Nile to form one distinct body of water.

The White Nile's source is Lake Victoria in Uganda, some 2,000 miles from the point where the two Niles come together. In Sudan, the river first passes through swampland and lagoons so overgrown with papyrus (a plant that was used to make the earliest form of paper) and other dense vegetation that the water seems to disappear. This enormous wetland area called the Sudd covers 6,370 square miles (16,492 sq. km) during the country's dry season in winter and grows to as many as 12,350 square miles (31,974 sq. km) in the wet summer season.

A VARIETY OF CLIMATES

Both the Libyan desert in the northwest and the Nubian desert in the north-central part of the country are harsh places where sand dunes and scorpions are plentiful but rain and vegetation are not. Water is precious in the country. Rich soil found in a small strip of land in the Nile Valley of northern Sudan comes to life when the annual flood materializes. In western Sudan, where there are no year-round streams, animals and people cannot venture far from the wells that support them.

The Geography of Sudan

Location: Northern Africa, bordering the Red Sea, between Egypt and Eritrea
Area: slightly more than one-fourth the size of the United States
    total: 967,494 square miles (2,505,810 sq km)
    land: 917,374 square miles (2,376,000 sq km)
    water: 50,120 square miles (129,810 sq km)
Borders: Central African Republic, 724 miles (1,165 km); Chad 845 miles (1,360 km); Democratic Republic of the Congo, 390 miles (628 km); Egypt, 791 miles (1,273 km); Eritrea, 376 miles (605 km); Ethiopia, 998 miles (1,606 km); Kenya, 144 miles (232 km); Libya, 238 miles (383 km); Uganda, 270 miles (435 km); coastline, 530 miles (853 km)
Climate: tropical in south; arid desert in north; rainy season (April to October)
Terrain: generally flat, featureless plain; mountains in east and west
Elevation extremes:
    lowest point: Red Sea 0 feet (0 meters)
    highest point: Kinyeti 10,456 feet (3,187 meters)
Natural hazards: dust storms, periodic persistent droughts

Source: Adapted from CIA World Factbook, 2002.

A sandstorm envelops buildings in Khartoum. The *haboob* is created by a hot, moist, strong wind that occurs along the southern edges of the Sahara. It may be accompanied by thunderstorms and small tornadoes.

Because Sudan is located in the tropics, temperatures are hot all year long. In Khartoum, where most of the country's population is clustered, temperatures can reach over 100° Fahrenheit (38° Celsius) in the summer. The high humidity makes the heat even harder to bear. Temperatures in the desert can climb to 110°F (43°C) in the summer, although on a winter night they will drop as low as 40°F (4°C). The southern portion of the country, which gets the most rainfall, has an average annual temperature of 86°F (30°C).

Annual rainfall in desert regions of the Sudan can be as little as 0.08 inches (0.2 cm). Direct sunlight and hot winds have dried out the soil in Sudan's desert areas, making it incapable of trapping the little rainfall that occurs. Since the soil cannot hold water, virtually nothing can grow in the desert.

Elsewhere, Sudan is composed of pastureland, green jungles, and forests. About 19 percent of the country is forest and woodland. In addition, about 46 percent of the country is permanent pastureland. Just 5 percent of Sudan's pastureland produces crops, though. The land is fertile, but the country suffers from severe droughts that have hampered crop production. Also, modern agricultural techniques are mostly unknown in Sudan, and irrigation is largely unavailable to Sudanese farmers. Erosion of farm soil has also had catastrophic effects on farming in the Sudan. The long-lasting civil war is at least partially responsible for this erosion, and for the unproductivity of what could be valuable farmland in Sudan. Soldiers burn crops, ruin the soil, and chase farmers off their land.

DUST STORMS IN THE TORRID ZONE

From May through July, people who pass through central Sudan may find themselves facing a wall of dust that totally blocks out the sun—some as high as 30,000 feet. These dramatic dust storms can last three or four days, making travel impossible. People who have been caught in the storms report that the blowing dust feels like sandpaper against their skin. Only camels, which have a third eyelid to protect themselves from the gritty sand, are untroubled by the storms.

The storms, known as *haboobs*, are named for the Arabic word for wind. A *haboob* generally begins in the Sahara Desert in Libya and Egypt and blows southeast into Sudan. The brisk desert winds pick up the sand from the dunes, carrying the grains through the air in a blinding storm. Astronomers say that similar storms sweep over the landscape on the planet Mars.

Haboobs are a symptom of dry land conditions and are prevalent in the Sudan because one quarter of its land is desert. The Sudan is one of the few countries in the world that experience these quickly moving dust storms.

Sudanese workers in front of a royal pyramid of Meroe, which is located in Sudan's northern desert some 186 miles (300 km) north of Khartoum. These were the tombs of kings and nobles who ruled over the area until A.D. 350.

History

Archaeological excavations along the Nile River in Sudan have uncovered the remnants of human civilization dating back 60,000 years or more. For much of recorded history, though, the people of Sudan have lived under the rule of others—Egyptians, Romans, Ethiopians, Ottoman Turks, or the British.

Starting in about 2000 B.C., Egyptian traders made their way along the Nile into northern Sudan. The Egyptians called the region Cush. It would continue to bear that name until the eighth century B.C., when the Egyptians would be driven out and the Nubians (as the indigenous people would become known) established their own independence.

Soon after arriving, the Egyptians established a series of forts in Cush to safeguard their traders. Among the treasures taken out of Cush by the Egyptians were jewels, ivory, incense, gold, and slaves. Eventually, Egyptian Pharaoh

Ahmose I, who ruled sometime between 1845 and 1500 B.C., declared Cush a province of Egypt.

By the eighth century B.C., the tables had turned. Internal conflicts in Egypt weakened the country and it was no longer able to dominate Cush. In fact, in 750 B.C. the Cushite king Kashta conquered portions of Egypt. Kashta and his successors would rule in Egypt for about 100 years. Taharqa, a Cushite king who lived from 688 to 663 B.C., withdrew from Egypt after losing a war to the Assyrians, an ancient people from Mesopotamia (modern-day Iraq) who had invaded Egypt.

THE MEROTIC CIVILIZATION

Having fled Egypt, the Nubians established their new capital in Sudan at Meroe, which is near present-day Shendi, a city on the Nile just north of Khartoum. Today, archaeologists are still uncovering new information about the wonders of the advanced civilization at Meroe, which was mentioned in the Bible as well as in the writings of the Greek historian Herodotus. This kingdom has left its imprint in modern Sudan in the crumbling remains of the temples and pyramids where its kings and queens worshiped and were buried.

The Nubian (or Merotic) civilization shared many similarities with the civilization in Egypt. Both cultures exerted influences on the other. Pottery and burial talismans found in the Sudan region predate similar discoveries made in Egypt. Meroe's 30-foot-high pyramids are not major tourist attractions, unlike the famous pyramids in Egypt, but more pyramids were built in Sudan than in Egypt. Initially, the two civilizations had similar languages and religions, but over time Meroe developed its own alphabet, a system of hieroglyphics, and a **pantheon** of gods. Its principal deity was Apedemak, the god of war and victory. He was depicted in **relief** carvings and statues as a creature with the body of a man and the head of a lion. Lions and elephants were both frequently depicted in Nubian art.

Living near the Nile, the Nubians were farmers who raised cotton, cattle, and the hardy grain called **millet** (all of these remain important crops in modern-day Sudan). Archaeologists have determined that these people also cultivated olive groves, tended sheep and goats, and ate the meat of gazelles, antelopes, and warthogs—animals no longer native to Sudan. The Nile River gave traders from Meroe access to other civilizations in the region, including those of Greece, Turkey, India, and the Arabian Peninsula. From Nubia such skills as ironworking spread into other parts of Africa.

The front panel of a chest from the Egyptian pharaoh Tutankhamen's tomb shows an Egyptian attack on the Nubians who once lived in the Sudan region.

Treasures of the Sand

In April 2002, Krzysztof Grzymski, a professor of archeology at the University of Toronto, and Tomasz Herbich, a Polish archeologist, discovered a royal palace and a colonnade buried deep in the sands of Meroe, about 124 miles from Khartoum. To uncover the ruins, Grzymski and Herbich used magneto-meters that employ the same technology used by hobbyists to locate coins on beaches. Until the two archaeologists made their discovery, much about the people, culture, and language of Meroe had not been explored because of the civil war in the Sudan.

"Here you've got this wonderful civilization that was literate, which extended over 1,000 miles, maybe more, up the Nile, and which built pyramids and palaces and temples and at the same time was a major center of iron pro-duction, and yet it is generally unknown to scholars and the general public," Grzymski said.

Using data fed from the magnetometer to a computer, archaeologists could "see" the remains of staircases and the street in front of the building, hints of what was to come when the actual digging commenced in the fall of 2002.

What they may find could match what was found 200 years ago at a pyra-mid near Meroe that was plundered by an Italian physician and fortune hunter known as Ferlini. When he blasted open the pyramid of Queen Amanishakheto he found exquisite gold amulets, rings, and necklaces. They were so beautiful that when he tried to sell them in Europe no one could believe that an African civilization had produced them. Collectors assumed they had to be fakes.

"There were jewels of great quality and beauty and often influenced by Greek art, which was really a surprise," Grzymski said. "People didn't expect deep in the heart of Africa depictions resembling those of Egyptian or classical Greek art."

More than a thousand inscriptions written in the Nubian language have been found but no one knows what they mean. Archaeologists have been able to figure out that the Nubians borrowed 24 Egyptian hieroglyphic symbols for their alphabet, but the puzzle of these ancient Merotic writings remains unsolved.

In 23 B.C. a Roman army, angry about Nubian incursions into Rome-occupied Egypt, invaded Meroe. Though the Romans ruled

Meroe indirectly during the next four centuries, the region would always be on the fringes of their empire. As Rome's power dwindled in the fourth century, the Romans finally withdrew. In about A.D. 350, Meroe was invaded by the Axumites an army from Abyssinia (modern-day Ethiopia), which destroyed the city of Meroe.

CHRISTIAN KINGDOMS

By the sixth century, the Sudan area once again became a center of trade and cultural exchange. Three kingdoms—Nobatia (also called Ballanah), Muqurra, and Alwa—shared the position Meroe once held as the center of power in the region. The rulers of these states had converted to Christianity, and the royal courts of all three were modeled on that of the ***Byzantine Empire***, the Christian eastern branch of the Roman Empire that dominated the Middle East region from Constantinople. These Christian kingdoms reached their high point during the ninth and tenth centuries.

The development of Islam during the seventh century had a major impact on the Middle East and Africa. Most historians believe that the northern Christian Nubian kingdoms, Nobatia and Muqurra, were forced to merge into a new, stronger state, Dunqulah, before the year 700 because of pressure from invading Arabs who wanted to spread their faith. Unlike other areas of the Middle East and Africa, the Christian Nubian kingdoms resisted the invasion of Islam and the Arab Muslims, although the conversion of much of Egypt to Islam cut off the Nubians from contact with the Byzantine Empire and Christian kingdoms in Europe.

Arab language and customs took root in the area long before Islam did, because the Nubians had to learn the Arabic language in order to trade with their neighbors. Arab-controlled Egypt established a strong relationship with the Nubian Christians, trading grain, slaves, horses, and manufactured goods for ivory, gold, gems, and cattle. Islam was spread gradually by Arab settlers who wandered into the region from Egypt, as well as by Muslim teachers who taught the new faith during their travels.

The Nubian kingdoms maintained their Christian beliefs until the 13th century. In 1276 the **Mamluks**, a powerful group of Arabs who ruled Egypt, helped overthrow the king of Dunqulah and place a new king on the throne. Though the new ruler was a Christian and Dunqulah remained nominally independent, the state was in essence controlled by the Mamluks. In 1315 the first Muslim king of Dunqulah took the throne. As Muslims gained power in the region, the Nubian Christian church declined. By the start of the 16th century most people in the Dunqulah region were members of the Muslim faith, and in 1517 the powerful Ottoman rulers of Turkey absorbed both Egypt and Dunqulah into their empire.

At the same time, in southern Nubia, the Christian kingdom of Alwa was fading as well. Alwa's ruling authority was replaced by the rule of the **Funj**, a strong race of black Africans who practiced Islam. The Funj would continue to rule the southern region until the 19th century. In east Sudan, meanwhile, another small Funj kingdom arose—the kingdom of Sennar, which thrived from the 16th to the 18th centuries. Sennar was a Muslim kingdom known as the Black Sultanate.

THREE THOUSAND EARS

Few men are hated long after they are dead. But the cold-blooded exploits of Muhammad Ali, an Ottoman warlord who ruled Egypt and conquered Sudan in the 19th century, have not been forgotten by the Sudanese, who still regard him as a villain.

By the end of the 18th century, most of Sudan was essentially a province of Egypt, which was part of the Ottoman Empire. However, Ottoman power in Egypt had become divided among rival Mamluk governors (called beys). The beys struggled for power until 1798, when a French army led by Napoleon Bonaparte invaded Egypt.

Though the Ottomans, with the help of Great Britain, forced the French to leave in 1801, the region entered a chaotic period. In 1805, the Ottomans appointed Muhammad Ali as the ruler of Egypt and told him to restore order. With the support of an Ottoman army, Ali eventually forced the Mamluks from control in Egypt. Many of the Mamluks retreated south into Sudan, where in 1811 they established a new state at Dunqulah as a base for slave trading.

The ambitious Ali wanted to break Egypt away from the Ottoman Empire (he has been called the "father of modern Egypt"). To do this he would need money and a strong military. In 1820 Ali's forces invaded Sudan, where he hoped to acquire gold and slaves to serve in his army. The Egyptian army, which was led by Ali's son Ismail, had two advantages: it was equipped with first-rate rifles

The Egyptian ruler Muhammad Ali (1769–1849) sent an army to occupy Sudan in 1820. This bloody conquest would result in 60 years of Egyptian political control over the country.

and the soldiers had a special incentive to be ruthless. They were to be paid a bounty for every human ear they sent back to Egypt. Ali soon amassed a collection of 3,000 ears.

Ismail was unable to give his father the gold he sought but had no trouble capturing slaves in the Sudan region. Thirty thousand slaves were soon forced to begin the journey northward to Cairo, but the trip through the desert was so difficult that half of the slaves died before they got to Egypt. Ismail himself was killed in Sudan by vengeful locals who set fire to his tent to pay him back for the atrocities he had committed. The man who led this attack was Mek Nimr, who became a national hero.

The war, though, was lost. Fifty thousand Sudanese had been killed by the time the Egyptians gained control of the land. Ali's invasion led to a 60-year period of Egyptian rule over Sudan (called the Turkiyah, or Turkish regime). This was a harsh rule. The Egyptians extracted high taxes and exploited the nomadic people of the region, who previously had been protected from invasion by the hills, swamps, and rainforest surrounding their home. The tusks of their elephants, the cattle they tended, and their very lives became valued commodities.

Ali did not start the slave trade in Sudan—slaves from Nubia had been incorporated into the Pharaohs' armies, and Sudanese slaves had served in the armies of Sennar. However, he did renew its vigor. Until the 1860s, slavery was the most profitable undertaking in Sudan. Slaves were exported, along with ivory and gum arabic (a substance used in cosmetics and inks). During the Turkiyah, Sudanese slave soldiers became part of units called *jihadiyya* that were stationed around the country to keep order or sent to such foreign areas as Greece and Arabia to fight their captors' battles.

There were some benefits from the occupation. Khartoum became the country's capital (as it remains today), and by the late

19th century the country enjoyed increased irrigation for farms and the introduction of new crops. A railroad was built, as were telegraph lines. During the 1850s the legal system in both Egypt and Sudan were revised, reducing the influence of Islamic *Sharia* courts by instituting a secular court system to hear most criminal cases. At the same time, though, the influence of Islam continued to spread as mosques and religious schools were built throughout the region.

THE MAHDI AND THE BRITISH

In 1869 the Suez Canal opened. This man-made waterway crossed Egypt to connect the Mediterranean Sea with the Red Sea and Indian Ocean. The Suez Canal soon became an important connection for Great Britain's colonial possessions in India and the Far East. To protect the canal, Britain became more involved in Egyptian affairs. However, the influence of the British threw the region into political turmoil. In 1882, the British occupied Egypt (though nominally the country remained part of the Ottoman Empire) and took over control of Sudan.

In Sudan, a charismatic figure named Muhammad Ahmed soon rebelled against British rule. Ahmed was a leader of an Islamic sect called Sammaniyah, which incorporated **Sufism**, a mystical form of the religion, with many local beliefs. He claimed to be the Mahdi, a prophet sent by Allah to prepare the people for the end of the world. The Mahdi preached a return to a strict early form of Islam, and many people were willing to follow him. In 1883, the Mahdi called for a holy war (or *jihad*) against Sudan's Egyptian and British occupiers. He achieved a series of impressive military victories beginning with his defeat of 7,000 Egyptian troops near Al Ubayyid.

A British general named Charles Gordon was sent to supervise the **Anglo-Egyptian** forces in Sudan. He was soon isolated in the walled city of Khartoum. The Mahdi and his soldiers besieged the city, cutting off supplies of food and other necessities. While General Gordon waited for reinforcements, the Mahdi tried to convince the British to surrender. Confident that help was on the way, General Gordon refused. He also refused the British government's demand that he leave the city (he could have escaped down the Nile River at any time), saying he was bound by honor to defend Khartoum.

Some 300 days into the siege, the Mahdi learned that a British force was only days away from reaching Khartoum. The Mahdi's men made an attack, broke into the city, and killed Gordon. The Mahdi's men then cut off his head, displaying it at the end of a spear in the center of Khartoum.

Two days after Khartoum fell to the Mahdi's men, the British reinforcements arrived, sized up the situation, and immediately withdrew from the area. The British did not return for 10 years.

Life under the Mahdi's rule brought a return to the fundamentals of Islam, but the Mahdi made some modifications to the religion. Instead of fulfilling the Muslim obligation to visit the holy city of Mecca, followers were encouraged to join the holy war. Instead of giving to the poor, which is also part of Islamic law, Muslims were told that their duty was to pay taxes to the state. Law and religious books were burned and courts enforced Islamic laws. In many of these ways, the government of the Mahdi was similar to that of the contemporary **Islamist** state of Sudan.

The Mahdi did not enjoy his authority for very long. He died from an infectious disease called typhus six months after the siege of Khartoum ended. His tomb in Omdurman, a city across the Nile from Khartoum where the Mahdi established his capital, is the most outstanding feature of the city. Omdurman hardly seemed worth fighting for—it was not much more than a collection of straw huts and mud dwellings. However, it remains the spiritual home of Islam in Sudan.

The British eventually returned to the Sudan in the 1890s under the leadership of Horatio Herbert Kitchener. He made careful plans to reassert British control throughout the region. An engineer by training, Kitchener built a railroad through the Nubian desert as quickly as possible under the most inhospitable conditions—high temperatures, dust storms, water shortages, and the ever-present possibility of enemy attack. The Sudan Military Railway progressed at a pace of one to three miles a day. Kitchener also had a plan for controlling the Nile in Sudan: spotlight-equipped gun boats that could travel up the river at 12 miles per hour while carrying a **howitzer** and an assortment of other big guns that far outclassed the weapons carried by the enemy.

It took 23 months for Kitchener's troops to advance to Omdurman, and then it was necessary to wait another month for the rains to swell the Nile so it would be deep enough for the gunships to be of use.

A 19th-century illustration shows British General Charles Gordon facing the Mahdi's warriors, who have broken into Khartoum. Gordon was killed defending the city in 1885.

The British forces—some 8,200 British troops as well as 17,600 Egyptian and Sudanese soldiers—had traveled 1,320 miles from Cairo. They brought with them 44 cannons, as well as a number of machine guns (called **Maxims**). One British officer who took part in the battle was 24-year-old Winston S. Churchill, who would later become prime minister of England. Churchill was attached to the 21st Lancers, who at Omdurman would take part in the last cavalry charge of the British army.

The Mahdi's successor, Khalifa Abdullah Ben Mohamed (*khalifa* is Arabic for "successor") prepared for the battle by building 17 forts and assembling some 40,000 men (called by their enemies "*dervishes*," a term which also means followers of the mystic Sufi form of Islam) to defend Omdurman. They were summoned to battle by the sound of an *ombeya*, a ceremonial instrument made from an elephant's trunk.

Charles Neufeld, a German engineer who was a prisoner of the Khalifa for more than a decade, described the dervishes as "nimble as cats and as bloodthirsty as a starving

The tomb of the Mahdi, in Omdurman, remains a shrine for Sudanese Muslims.

man-eating tiger, utterly regardless of their own lives, and capable of continuing stabbing and jabbing with spear and sword while carrying half a dozen wounds, any one of which would have put a European ***hors de combat***."

The superior firepower of Kitchener's gunboats inflicted severe damage on the Khalifa's forts and the dervishes were further demoralized by the damage their opponents inflicted on the Mahdi's tomb. As one observer wrote, "The people were dumfounded; their shouting ceased, even the neighing of the horses was stilled, and at the sunset prayer I could not hear the first 'God is the most great' from the leader."

Churchill, who was there as both soldier and journalist, wrote, "I was, I think, the first to see the enemy, certainly the first to hear their bullets. Never shall I see such a sight again. At the very least there were 40,000 men—five miles long in lines with great humps and squares at intervals—and I can assure you that when I heard them shouting their war songs from my coign of vantage on the ridge of Heliograph Hill, I and my little patrol felt very lonely. And though I never doubted the issue—I was in great awe."

The Muslim dervishes fought bravely, believing that their faith in the Prophet Muhammad would make them immune to the English bullets. Nonetheless, they were mowed down by the better-equipped British soldiers. During the first five hours of fighting, the Khalifa lost 11,000 men while just 48 of Kitchener's men were killed and 400 wounded. When all was lost, the Khalifa fled, bringing to an end the checkered history of the rule by the Mahdi and his successor. Their reign had been marked by hundreds of thousands of deaths from famine, disease, and fighting over religious restrictions.

With the Khalifa defeated, the British and Egyptians established a joint rule (the ***condominium***) over the Sudan, although the British had much more say in how the country was run. The condominium brought about a prosperous and peaceful period

Great Britain sent soldiers from other parts of its empire—including the members of the Ninth Bengal Cavalry pictured here—to fight in the British reconquest of Sudan. Britain started fighting in Sudan in 1896, after first subduing Egypt; by September 1898 the Khalifa's army had been crushed at Omdurman.

from 1899 to 1955, but the seeds of eventual discord in Sudan were sown during this time. Many historians and political scientists argue that modern Sudan is prone to military rule because of the tradition of Sudanese military leadership established during the condominium period. The British allowed the Sudanese to serve as officers in the military, a practice that was not permitted in other parts of the British empire.

In addition, the British rulers treated the northern and southern areas of the country differently, which has directly contributed to the divisions felt by the north and south today. While the British modernized northern Sudan by expanding telegraph and rail services into more of those areas, it made no such attempt in the south. To help the economy of Sudan, the government created the Geizra Scheme, an agricultural and irrigation project near Sennar in the north where cotton was grown for export to Britain. At the same time, believing that the south was not ready for modernization, the British sealed the area off from outsiders and issued laws that prohibited northerners from working or traveling there. The British discouraged the black African tribesmen of the southern Sudan from adopting Islam, speaking Arabic, or dressing like their northern countrymen. Instead they encouraged the spread of Christianity and allowed Christian missionaries to enter the area and establish churches and schools. Meanwhile, southerners enjoyed more freedom to lead their own people.

INDEPENDENCE AND STRIFE

Though generally peaceful, life during the condominium period was not perfect. The end of World War I in 1918 brought an end to the Ottoman Empire and its control of Muslim Arab lands in the Middle East and Africa. In many of these countries independence movements began; Sudan was no exception. Arab nationalists from the northern part of Sudan wished for freedom from British control, and advocated a unified Sudan.

In 1921 Ali Abd al Latif, a Muslim Dinka and former officer in the British army, founded the United Tribes Society. This organization (later called the White Flag League) called for an independent Sudan in which tribal and religious leaders would share power. In

1924, demonstrations led by the White Flag League challenged the British colonial presence. However, Abd al Latif's arrest and subsequent exile stalled the nationalist movement.

In 1936 Egypt and Britain signed a treaty that set a timetable for the end of British rule in the region. However, the treaty did not address what would happen to Sudan. This worried Sudanese nationalists, who feared the northern part of Sudan might become attached to Egypt, while the southern region would be claimed by African neighbors like Uganda and Kenya. World War II (1939–1945)

interrupted the debate on Sudanese independence, but by the late 1940s the issue had been raised again. In February 1953, Egypt and Great Britain signed an agreement setting a three-year transition period for self-government in Sudan. On January 1, 1956, Sudan became an independent republic.

There was trouble right from the start. Even before independence, in August 1955 a military unit composed of southerners mutinied at Torit. Many of the mutineers dispersed into the countryside with their weapons and began waging guerrilla war in southern Sudan.

Sudan's legislative assembly meets in Khartoum to discuss independence, 1951. Pressure by nationalists would eventually lead to self-government for Sudan.

> **Since Sudan's independence in 1956 there have been three democratically elected governments. All were short-lived.**

This war would continue on and off for the next 17 years.

Also, though the Sudanese had selected a democratic parliament in 1956, the civilian government was soon overthrown by a military *coup* led by two generals, Ibrahim Abbud and Ahmad Abd al Wahab. By 1959, Abbud had complete control of the government.

Opposition to the Abbud regime remained, in particular because of Abbud's policy toward the southern part of the country. He tried to suppress the culture and religious beliefs of people in the region by imposing those of the Arab and Islamic north. The Abbud government had to contend with the civil war, which was led by guerrilla forces known as the Anya Nya (this name comes from a poisonous drink). Other groups, such as the Sudanese Communist Party and a leftist group calling itself the United National Front, also caused problems for the Abbud government. After rioting by students, civil servants, and trade unionists in October 1964, Abbud dissolved the military regime and reinstituted a civilian government, operating under the 1950s transitional constitution. Sirr al-Khatim al-Khalifa was named prime minister, and a 15-seat parliament was selected to prepare a new constitution.

Elections were held in March 1965, but continuing unrest in the south prevented many people from voting. The elected coalition government, led by Muhammad Ahmad Mahjub, cracked down on communists and the southern guerrillas. However, by July 1966 Mahjub was forced to resign because of a dispute that split his coalition government. A majority of the parliament supported Sadiq al-Mahdi, the son of the country's Islamic religious leader. Sadiq al-Mahdi was opposed to religious rule in Sudan; he offered plans for economic development and to grant greater freedoms to those living in southern Sudan. His government soon lost public confidence, however, and by the end of 1967 the Mahdi coalition had collapsed. Mahjub returned to power as prime minister.

The unrest continued. In 1969, a military dictator named Jaafar al-Nimeri seized control of northern Sudan. By this time some 500,000 people had been killed in the southern civil war. Nimeri increased the number of government troops in southern Sudan, and began to bring in tanks, MIG aircraft, and other weapons from the Soviet Union to forcibly control the southerners.

By 1971 a guerrilla leader named Joseph Lagu, a well-educated former captain in the Sudanese Army, had become the leader of the southern opposition (now renamed the Southern Sudan Liberation Movement, or SSLM), which controlled southern Sudan. Nimeri hoped to end the civil war and reunify the country, so he opened negotiations with Lagu. After a conference at Addis Ababa, Ethiopia, mediated by Emperor Haile Selassie, the two sides

Jaafar al-Nimeri assumed power in Sudan in 1969, and ruled as a military-supported dictator until 1985. During Nimeri's regime he agreed to a peace accord with the leaders of southern Sudan; however, after the peace failed in 1984 Nimeri was removed from office.

reached an agreement. The Addis Ababa accords, signed in March 1972, provided for a cease-fire and gave the southern region autonomy under the Sudanese government.

Ten years of peace followed the Addis Ababa accords. However, Nimeri's popularity waned after some of his important economic initiatives failed due to corruption and incompetence. The dictator had a dream of making the Sudan a "breadbasket to the world" by building the Jongelei Canal to divert water from the Sudd wetlands to the Gezira area. To get the money to finance the proposed canal, Nimeri borrowed heavily from foreign countries, plunging his country into debt. The canal was never finished.

As Nimeri's support base evaporated he made a fateful alliance with the National Islamic Front (NIF), a group of Muslim **fundamentalists** that previously had not enjoyed popular support in the country. He stunned the south in 1983 by making Muslim law (*Sharia*) the law of Sudan. To demonstrate Islam's intolerance for alcohol, Nimeri had whiskey bottles emptied

John Garang, leader of the Sudanese People's Liberation Army (SPLA), in a 1992 photo. Born in 1945 into a Christian Dinka family, Garang went to college in the United States, ultimately earning a Ph.D. in agricultural economics. He also received military training at Fort Benning, Georgia—training that has helped him fight a guerrilla war against the Muslim-dominated government of Sudan since 1983.

into the Nile. He introduced *Sharia* punishments for simple crimes. Thieves could have their hands cut off, for example.

As a result, civil war broke out once again in the south, this time coordinated by the Sudanese People's Liberation Movement (SPLM) and its military arm, the Sudanese People's Liberation Army (SPLA). The conflict soon turned into a full-scale civil war. During 1984, the SPLA was able to take control of many rural southern districts. The resurgence of fighting, and Nimeri's unpopularity, led in 1985 to the overthrow of his government by the army. A transitional government, led by Lieutenant General Abd ar Rahman Siwar adh Dhahab, was created. Siwar adh Dhahab wanted Sudan to have a democratic government and called for free elections in 1986. When the people went to the polls they returned Sadiq al-Mahdi to power.

The Mahdi government failed to make progress in ending the civil war or in solving the country's economic problems. Sadiq al-Mahdi hesitated to withdraw *Sharia* as the law of Sudan, so the fighting continued. In 1989, on the day that Sadiq al-Mahdi intended to abolish *Sharia*, his government was overthrown in a coup planned by Hassan al-Turabi, the leader of the National Islamic Front, and carried out by General Omar Hassan al-Bashir. Bashir charged that Mahdi had "wasted the country's time and squandered its energies with much talk and policy vacillation."

Bashir declared **martial law**. He banned political parties and labor unions and reinstituted such *Sharia* punishments as floggings and public amputations. By 1990 the National Congress Party, a political arm of the National Islamic Front, had gained

> Michael Horowitz of the Hudson Institute, an Indianapolis-based social policy organization, has described Sudan as "the Hitler regime of our time" because of its human rights violations.

significant power in Sudan's parliament. In 1990–91, Turabi formed an organization for militants, the Popular Arab Islamic Conference (PAIC), which was based in Khartoum. This group opposed the 1991 Gulf War against Iraq, and allowed anti-western Islamists to operate freely in Sudan. The most notorious example is Osama bin Laden, who trained terrorists in Sudan until 1996, when the U.S. pressured the Sudanese government to expel him. Two years later, in 1998, U.S. forces destroyed a pharmaceutical factory in Khartoum with suspected ties to bin Laden. Believing that the factory was manufacturing nerve gas components, and in retaliation for two recent attacks on U.S. embassies in East Africa that killed 12 Americans and 300 Africans, U.S. ships on the Red Sea launched dozens of cruise missiles at the al-Shifa plant.

Bashir continues to rule the Sudan today. His biggest adversary

Angry about Sudan's support of the terrorists who had carried out the August 7, 1998, attacks on the U.S. embassies in Tanzania and Kenya, on August 20, 1998, the United States launched cruise missiles at targets in Sudan and Afghanistan, including suspected terrorist training camps and the al-Shifa pharmaceutical plant, which was believed to be making chemical or biological weapons.

remains John Garang, a former Sudanese colonel educated in the U.S. who heads the Sudan People's Liberation Movement. The SPLM has been waging war with the government since 1983. Some concessions have been made to the south, but not enough to end the fighting. In 1991, for example, Bashir absolved the south from following Sharia while keeping the Islamic laws in place in the north. The SPLM was unhappy with having Sharia laws anywhere in the country. In 1998, both sides agreed in principle to southern self-determination through a **referendum** that could be independently monitored by other countries. But the details of the agreement were never finalized and the referendum was never held. The two sides have been unable to reach agreement on where the border should be between the north and south. In the meantime, the situation in Sudan became even worse in 1998–99 when famine killed an estimated 70,000 people.

In October 2002, the Sudanese Government and SPLA rebels agreed to a cease-fire while representatives of the two sides met in Kenya to discuss a peaceful settlement to the long-running conflict. The international community hailed this cessation of hostilities as an important step toward peace.

Altogether, more than 2 million people have been killed by war, disease, and famine, according to a 2002 report by the U.S. Committee for Refugees. The report also found that some 500,000 Sudanese have fled the country and are now living as refugees in other countries, and that slave raids are still occurring on a regular basis in parts of southern Sudan.

Omar al-Bashir (left) and Hassan al-Turabi gesture to the crowd during a military parade in Khartoum, 1995. The two men shared power in Sudan from 1989 to 1999, when Bashir dissolved parliament. Turabi was arrested by Bashir's police in February 2001 and remained in custody for more than two years.

Politics, the Economy, and Religion

Since Sudan received its independence from Great Britain and Egypt in 1956, the country has been struggling with civil war and a succession of Islamic military dictatorships. Today, the government is run by a military ***junta*** that took power in 1989, and has strong support from the Islamist National Congress Party (NCP), the political arm of the National Islamic Front.

The current president of Sudan, Omar al-Bashir, has dictatorial authority over the government. He has never been hesitant to wield his power; in December 1999 he partially suspended the country's constitution and dissolved parliament over a split with his former ally, Hassan al-Turabi.

Bashir and Turabi had shared power in the country since 1989 but their partnership grew uneasy in 1998 when Bashir's second-in-command, vice president Muhammad

Salih al-Zubayr, was killed in an airplane crash. Turabi, who was speaker of the parliament, tried to increase his own power by amending Sudan's constitution to limit the president's authority. In response Bashir dissolved parliament and took other measures to preserve his rule and restrict Turabi's. Though parliament has since been reconvened, measures have been taken to extend Bashir's power beyond the end of his current term as president.

POWER IN THE HANDS OF THE PRESIDENT

The Sudanese constitution, adopted in 1998, gives most of the political power to the president. As head of government and chief of state, the president commands the military, appoints judges, and rules over a cabinet that oversees various departments of government. The president has the power to make laws, and can even amend the constitution.

The presidency is an elective office, and presidents serve five-year terms. In the most recent election, held in 2000, Bashir received more than 86 percent of the vote. However, most independent observers believe the elections were rigged, and all of Sudan's opposition parties boycotted the election because there were no guarantees the process would be "free and fair."

A provision in the current constitution limits a president to two terms, and Bashir is currently serving his second elected term. However, in April 2002 Sudan's National Assembly passed a constitutional amendment that could allow Bashir to run for a third term when his current term ends in 2005.

Two vice presidents serve under the president. The president is also served by the Council of Ministers. Each member of this cabinet is in charge of a department of the government. The Council is dominated by Bashir's allies—former military officers and members of the National Congress—although he has appointed some opposition leaders to cabinet positions.

Sudan's current flag was adopted in 1968 and first hoisted in 1970. The flag incorporates the pan-Arab colors used in the 1916 Arab Revolt, and has a design similar to that of the Arab Revolt flag (that banner had a red triangle and black-green-white stripes). The flag of Sudan is also similar to the flags of several other Arab countries— Jordan, Kuwait, and the United Arab Emirates.

Laws in Sudan are the responsibility of the National Assembly. According to the constitution, three-fourths of the members of this parliament are supposed to be elected to four-year terms by the people, with the remainder appointed by the president. According to the 1998 constitution, this is to ensure "representation of women and scientific and professional classes." However, most observers recognize that the National Assembly is not truly a democratically elected legislative body. While some Sudanese have boycotted the polls because they feel elections are rigged, many others cannot vote because of the ongoing civil war in their provinces. During the last national election, in 2000, fighting in the south prevented voting in three of Sudan's 26 states, so President Bashir appointed people to represent those states in the National Assembly.

As a result, the assembly is dominated by members of the National Congress Party; of the 360 seats in the National Assembly, 355 are held by NCP members.

At the top of Sudan's judicial system is a Supreme Court, which is headed by a chief justice. A group of judges, known as the Supreme Council of the Judiciary, supervises the operation of lower courts—courts of first instance and appellate courts. In addition,

Special Revolutionary Courts are military courts that oversee the trials of revolutionaries or enemies of the current government.

Sudan's 26 states are each controlled by a governor, elected for a four-year term, and an elected state assembly.

A WEAK ECONOMY

Sudan is a poor country with few paved roads, an inadequate water supply, a shortage of skilled labor, and little arable land. Add to the mix a civil war, unchecked immigration from neighboring countries, and frequent droughts and famines, and it is easy to see why the economy has suffered. In Sudan, **inflation** and high prices are directly linked to the country's many problems.

To build the country's economy, over the past four decades Sudan has borrowed money from other nations, as well as from an agency known as the International Monetary Fund (IMF). The IMF has existed since 1944, when it was created at a meeting in New Hampshire attended by representatives from 44 countries. Today, the IMF has 181 member states and funding of $220 billion a year. The agency is not without its critics, however, who argue that half of the underdeveloped countries that received loans from it over a 30-year period are no better off today than they were before they took the IMF's money.

Sudan's relationship with the IMF has been stormy. By 1985, agricultural and industrial projects facilitated by the fund and another international lending organization, the World Bank, had yet to get off the ground and the country's factories were producing at about half their capacity. Food production that year was half of what it had been in 1960, and famine was widespread in the south and west. In addition, the government owed $9 billion in international debt and was unwilling to follow the economic measures the IMF insisted that it take. As a result, the IMF declared Sudan bankrupt in 1986. In 1990 it labeled Sudan "non-cooperative." Three years later the fund threatened to expel Sudan unless it agreed to make more regular payments on its debt and take other fiscal measures. It suspended Sudan's voting rights in the IMF, a privilege that all member nations have.

In 1997, Sudan began implementing the economic policies proposed by the International Monetary Fund. These stabilized both inflation and the currency exchange rate. Pleased with progress the country was making, by 2000 the IMF had restored Sudan to full membership. However, as of mid-2002 Sudan still owed the International Monetary Fund nearly $2 billion.

The Economy of Sudan

Gross domestic product (GDP*): $12.07 billion

Per capita income: $330

Inflation: 10%

Natural resources: petroleum; small reserves of iron ore, copper, chromium ore, zinc, tungsten, mica, silver, gold, hydropower

Agriculture (43% of GDP): cotton, groundnuts (peanuts), sorghum, millet, wheat, gum arabic, sugarcane, cassara, mangos, papaya, bananas, sweet potatoes, sesame; sheep, livestock

Industry (17% of GDP): soap distilling, shoes, petroleum refining, pharmaceuticals, armaments

Services (40% of GDP): government services, other

Foreign trade:

Imports—$1.6 billion: foodstuffs, manufactured goods, machinery and transport equipment, medicines and chemicals, textiles.

Exports—$2.1 billion: oil and petroleum products, cotton, sesame, livestock, groundnuts, gum arabic, sugar.

Currency exchange rate: 260 Sudanese dinars = $1 U.S. (October 2002)

*GDP, or gross domestic product, is the total value of goods and services produced in a country annually. All figures are 2001 estimates unless otherwise noted.
Sources: CIA World Factbook, 2002; World Bank; U.S. Department of State FY 2001 Country Commercial Guide.

THE IMPORTANCE OF OIL

Sudan's most promising natural resource is oil, which was first discovered in 1978. However, the country has not been able to take advantage of the economic potential of this resource until relatively recently, as a pipeline from the oil fields to Port Sudan was not completed until 1999. By 2002 oil generated more than $500 million in annual income for the country. Major oil companies from Malaysia, China, Sweden, Austria, France, and Canada have partnered with Sudan to extract the oil.

The discovery of oil has been a mixed blessing. The government

Civilian refugees walk with their belongings through the village of Nhialdiu, in southern Sudan, August 2001. These were among the thousands displaced by fighting in the area just south of Bentiu, where oil companies, supported by the government, maintain oil facilities. The expansion of an oil pipeline in the area, and increases in oil production, have led to bombing by the government to clear thousands of civilians from the area.

has used money from oil to help pay its costs to continue fighting the southern rebels. Some of this money has also been used to start new industries that support the war (for example, manufacturers of weapons and munitions). Also, the government in Khartoum has pursued a scorched-earth policy against the people who live where the oil is located. After visiting Sudan in October 2001, the administrator of the United States Agency for International Development, Andrew Natsios, said, "Oil has only helped to fuel tension, bitterness and war. . . . The abandoned and destroyed villages were readily apparent as we flew over the pipeline. The destruction of people's lives could not be more apparent."

In November 2001 a $1 billion class-action lawsuit was filed against Talisman Energy of Calgary, Canada, one of the oil companies operating in the area. The Presbyterian Church of Sudan and several co-plaintiffs accused Talisman Energy of having "deliberately and intentionally facilitated, conspired in, or aided and abetted in the use of Sudanese armed forces in a brutal ethnic cleansing campaign against a civilian population based on their ethnicity and religion for the purpose of enhancing its ability to explore and extract oil from areas of southern Sudan."

The lawsuit alleged that Talisman pays the government to protect its oil operations and the government in turn uses its military forces to wage a brutal campaign against religious and ethnic minorities in the oil-rich areas.

Among the people caught in the crossfire are the Nuba, who live in a 30,000-square-mile area in southern Kordofan. They live in the geographical center of Sudan where the oil has been found and in an area also blessed with rich soil that could be farmed to feed many people.

Before war came to their isolated homes, the Nuba people had enjoyed the most beautiful scenery in the country and a heritage uninfluenced by outsiders. One of the facets of their unique culture was the practice of not wearing clothing. This was regarded as an embarrassment by the Muslim government in Khartoum.

The government has been trying to eliminate the Nuba people since 1985—even Nubas who are Muslims. Civilians have been bombed, scores of villages destroyed, fields of food ruined, and tens of thousands of Nubas relocated to internment areas euphemistically called "peace camps."

In January 2002, the government agreed to a ceasefire in the region negotiated by the U.S. special envoy to Sudan, John Danforth. An international monitoring unit has been formed to see that the ceasefire is enforced.

FARMING AND INDUSTRY

Agriculture is the country's greatest strength. It represents 43 percent of the nation's gross domestic product (GDP), which is the market value of all goods and services produced in a country during a one-year period. Eighty percent of Sudanese workers make their livings farming. Cotton, peanuts, sesame seeds, and grains like sorghum, millet, and wheat are grown—both for use in the country and for export. Saudi Arabia, one of the countries that provided significant investment funds during the 1970s to projects intended to make Sudan the "breadbasket" of the world, purchases about a quarter of Sudan's food exports.

Sudan is the second-largest producer of gum arabic, a product of the Acacia tree. The resin can be used to replace oil in low-fat baked goods, to thicken candies, in the adhesive on postage stamps, and to stabilize the foam in beer and soda. Before the civil war, Sudan had been the world's top producer of gum arabic but now it shares the market with the neighboring country of Chad. Chad began processing the resin at the urging of food and cosmetic industry users, who feared instability in Sudan would prevent them from obtaining this key ingredient in their products.

Industry makes up 17 percent of Sudan's GDP. This aspect of the country's economy is dominated by the processing of agricultural products, such as sugar and cotton. Cement, soap, shoe manufacturing, and petroleum production round out the list of the country's biggest industries. Industrial plants are both government and privately owned.

The United States does a small amount of trade with Sudan. According to official U.S. figures for 2002, American companies sent $9 million in goods to Sudan, while Sudan exported just $345,000 in materials to the United States.

Overall, however, the economic forecast for Sudan seems to be improving. A trade imbalance has historically been a problem for Sudan—the country imported far more goods than it exported. By 2002, however, the value of exports was greater than the value of imported goods. And while the inflation rate in Sudan was estimated at 10 percent in 2001—a relatively high rate compared to Western nations like the United States—inflation is far less than it was ten years earlier in 1991, when the rate was 300 percent.

A group of young men harvest a field of cotton in the Gezira region. Farming is the most important part of Sudan's economy; about 80 percent of the population make their living from agriculture.

THE IMPORTANCE OF ISLAM

According to Sudan's 1998 constitution, people are free to worship as they please. Article 24 of the constitution states, "Every human being shall have the right of freedom of conscience and religious creed [and the right to] manifest the same by way of worship, education, practice or performance of rites or ceremonies; and no one shall be coerced to adopt such faith as he does not believe in, nor to practice rites or services he does not voluntarily consent to." However, the constitution also establishes Islamic law as the basis for legislation in Sudan, and says that Islam is the guiding religion for most of the population. About 70 percent of Sudanese are Muslims; most of these live in the northern part of the country.

Islam dates from the seventh century, when a 40-year-old Arab

A Sudanese woman displays her veil and head covering in El Obeid.

trader named Muhammad began receiving messages from Allah (God). Allah's messages were written in the Qur'an (also called the Koran). These included the laws and guidelines for the Islamic faith. (The word *Islam* comes from the Arabic verb *aslama*, which means "submission to God.")

To accept Islam is to accept five basic laws: *shahada*, the tenet that there is one god, Allah, and that Muhammad was his prophet; *salat*, the duty of Muslims to pray five times a day; *sawm*, the celebration of Ramadan, the holy month in which it is necessary to fast from sunup to sundown; *zakat*, a tradition of charitable donation; and *hajj*, the requirement that Muslims make a pilgrimage to Mecca, the birthplace of Islam.

Sharia, the law of Islam, spells out the moral goals of a community and covers a Muslim's religious, political, social, and private life. It is based on the Qur'an, the Sunna (an early interpretation of the Qur'an written by Muhammad's followers), and other Islamic writings and traditions. In Sudan's Islamic society, the courts look to *Sharia* for guidance when interpreting the law and enforcing justice.

Islamic nations vary in the strictness in which they apply the *Sharia* to their societies. One of the most familiar examples of *Sharia* law in Arab countries is the custom requiring women to keep their faces covered in public. And in many nations under Islamic law, people who violate *Sharia* risk brutal consequences. Lawbreakers in Islamic countries may be stoned, whipped, or killed. In Sudan, for example, the sentence for armed robbery is the amputation of the right hand and left foot.

Sharia applies to all residents of the northern part of Sudan— even non-Muslims—and is often applied in the southern areas of the country as well. The case of Abok Alfa Abok provides an example. In 2002 Abok, a pregnant 18-year-old Christian Dinka woman, was tried and convicted of adultery in the southwestern state of

Darfur. Her sentence: death by stoning. When she appealed, the death sentence was commuted. Instead, Abok was ordered to be flogged with 75 lashes, to be delivered after her baby was born. At her trial Abok did not have a lawyer; nor did she understand the Arabic language spoken by prosecutors during her trial. Sudan's justice minister, Ali Mohamed Osman Yassin, admitted to international reporters that he thought the death sentence was both excessive and cruel. Yet he maintained that harsh Islamic penalties deter people from committing crimes. "Flogging is a humiliating punishment because it is painful and degrading. People try to avoid it and therefore crimes that result in flogging are curtailed," Yassin said.

OTHER RELIGIONS IN SUDAN

While Muslims in the north account for a majority of Sudan's population, the country is also home to Christians and **animists**, people who follow African tribal religions that worship nature.

Christianity has a long tradition in Sudan, dating back to ancient times. In fact, the Christian kingdoms of present-day Sudan were among the few in the region able to resist the spread of Islam during the centuries when the new religion spread throughout North Africa and the Middle East. Today, however, Christians account for a mere 5 percent of Sudan's population.

Though the constitution says that people are free to follow other religions, such as Christianity, according to *Sharia* any adult Muslim who converts from Islam to Christianity (or any other faith) and refuses to convert back again should be put to death. And the Muslim-dominated government has focused its attention on Arabizing and Islamicizing the black Christians in the south.

The civil war has been condemned by Christians worldwide. In the spring of 2002, more than 150 American Christian religious and political leaders issued a statement which said in part that the torment "suffered by faith communities of Sudan . . . may be more brutal, more

Dinka boys and their families participate in a Christian service at a refugee camp in northern Kenya. The ongoing civil war and Muslim persecution have forced Sudanese Christians like these to flee their homes in southern Sudan.

systematic, more deliberate, more implacable and more purely genocidal than those taking place anywhere in the world today."

Animists—those who believe that things in nature, such as trees or animals, have a consciousness—are also persecuted by the Muslim government of Sudan. African tribal religions are practiced by about 20 percent of Sudanese, mostly in the south. Members of the Dinka and Nuer tribes, who still live in mud huts, believe that when things go wrong it is because the gods are unhappy. For example, if a couple had trouble conceiving a baby they would consult a tribal elder for guidance on pleasing the gods. Because the lack of rain can be deadly for agriculture-based people, there are rituals for bringing rain. The spirits of ancestors are believed to affect the daily lives of tribe members.

Children sit beneath an SPLA flag in the Lumon area of Sudan. Sadly, the decades of civil war have deeply divided the people of Sudan.

The People

There are more than 37 million people living in Sudan but because they come from so many different ethnic and religious backgrounds it is difficult to pinpoint a typical Sudanese. About 52 percent of the people are black and 39 percent Arab. The Beja, nomadic camel and goat herders who have been living in Eastern Sudan for 4,000 years, make up about 6 percent of the population. Foreigners and members of other ethnic groups make up the remaining 3 percent.

In 2001, President Bashir made an unusual request of Muslim males. He urged them to take more wives in order to increase the population and to help Sudan overcome severe labor shortages. *Sharia* laws allow Muslim men to have four wives at one time. Of course, at the same time that Bashir was urging people to have more babies, his government continued to kill and displace southern civilians.

Life in Sudan varies widely. Most citizens speak Arabic,

and many also speak English and other languages. Some Sudanese live in cities and have office jobs, while others live in mud huts and survive by hunting, fishing, and raising crops. The civil war has caused many people to flee their homes and settle in refuge camps.

In the north, which is predominantly Muslim, men wear long gowns called *jalabiyyas*. They cover their heads in either white or orange skull caps or white turbans called *emmas*. These turbans are made by wrapping six feet of white fabric carefully around their heads. Women traditionally wear a fabric garment, called a *tobe*, which is ten yards long; they wrap these *tobes* around their heads and bodies, obscuring the dresses they wear underneath. The *tobes* may be white, dark, or brightly colored. The traditional veils often seen in other Islamic countries are less common in Sudan.

Muslim men are considered the heads of their households and spend considerable time socializing with other men rather than with their wives. Women generally eat only after the men in the family have done so and men have the freedom to meet other men in cafes and marketplaces called *souks*. These open-air locations are where Sudanese can buy the

The People of Sudan

Population: 37,090,298
Ethnic groups: black 52%, Arab 39%, Beja 6%, foreigners 2%, other 1%
Religions: Sunni Muslim 70% (in north), indigenous beliefs 25%, Christian 5% (mostly in south and Khartoum)
Age structure:
    0–14 years: 44.2%
    15–64 years: 53.6%
    65 years and over: 2.2%
Population growth rate: 2.73%
Birth rate: 37.21 births/1,000 population
Death rate: 9.81 deaths/1,000 population
Infant mortality rate: 67.14 deaths/ 1,000 live births
Life expectancy at birth:
    total population: 57.33 years
    males: 56.22 years
    females: 58.5 years
Total fertility rate: 5.22 children born/woman
Literacy: 46.1% (1995 est.)

All figures are 2002 estimates unless otherwise indicated.
Source: CIA World Factbook, 2002

This map shows the distribution of Sudan's population. Though with 37 million people Sudan is one of the most populous countries of the Arab world, with an average population density of 32 people per square mile (14 per sq. km) it is much less crowded than North African neighbors Egypt (169 people per square mile; 75/sq. km) Tunisia (143/sq. mile; 62/sq. km) and Morocco (108/sq. mile; 47/sq. km).

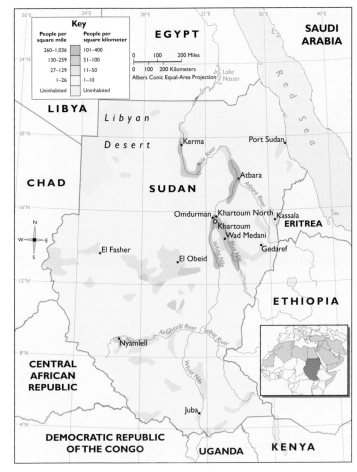

material for *tobes* and *jalabiyyas* and purchase leather goods, jewelry, cooking utensils, and other items made by local craftsmen. Sudanese Muslim women run the household and take care of the children.

ANCIENT RITUALS PERSIST

When some Muslim girls in Sudan are about 12 years old they are ritually circumcised by midwives. The surgery involves cutting off part or all of the girls' external genitals. Not only does the practice make sexual pleasure impossible for a woman but it can also lead to shock, bleeding, and other complications.

Ritual circumcision is not unique to Sudan. It is practiced

A woman sorts grain in the village of Acheran, located in the Nuba Mountains.

throughout Africa and the Middle East even though there are laws against this inhumane practice. The World Health Organization estimates that 130 million girls and women in 28 countries have been circumcised. Legislation in Sudan prohibits ritual circumcision, but the custom is so deeply ingrained that it continues. Some families believe their daughter will not marry if she does not have the surgery.

Children in the south also face traditional rituals that westerners might consider barbaric. In the Dinka tribe, for instance, a seven- or eight-year-old boy has six lower teeth removed from his mouth with the aid of sharp sticks. He is given nothing to ease the pain and warned not to cry.

At about the age of 12, when he is considered a man in the tribe, his face is sometimes scarred. The scars are made with a long, sharp knife on the forehead. Boys who cry are humiliated by the tribe.

Another adolescent tribal ritual is the *toc*. This is a contest to see which boy can drink the most milk. Each boy participating is responsible for drinking all of the milk from a certain number of cows as the contest plays out over seven months. During that time the boys can do nothing but drink milk until the day the contest is decided by a tribal vote that determines which boy is the fattest. Former basketball star Manute Bol, who grew up in Sudan, recalled his childhood brush with the *toc* this way. "I got up to 250 pounds, I guess, but it is weight you lose very quickly," Bol recalled.

"Especially in the summer because it is so hot. My cousin, he got so as he could not walk. This is true. He weighed over 600 pounds. His legs were so fat, so close together, he could not walk."

In some tribes like the Dinka, cows are considered much more than farm animals. They represent wealth and prestige. A man is judged by the size of his herd and when a woman is to be betrothed, her husband-to-be's family must offer his future father-in-law a **dowry** of cows. Once, a bride could fetch as much as 100 cows from her suitor's family. Today, however, with few families in the south having many cows, the dowry negotiations are merely promises of cows that may never be fulfilled.

Cows are rarely slaughtered for food. Instead, southern cattle herders find many uses for cows. They obtain milk and butter, of course, but also cow urine is used to wash clothes, dye hair, and tan hides. Even the cow's excrement is put to use. Dung fires produce ash that can be applied to cattle to protect them from ticks. Rubbed on skin, cow dung serves as body art and, when made into a paste, it keeps teeth clean.

SLAVES AND REFUGEES

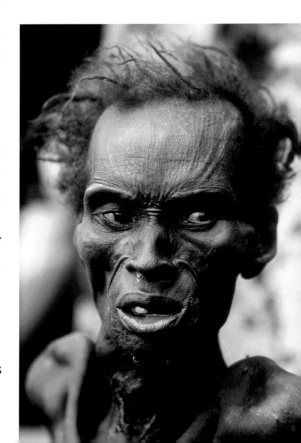

Another ancient practice that persists in Sudan is slavery. No one is certain how many slaves there are in Sudan. U.S. Secretary of State Colin L. Powell has said that the number of people enslaved today throughout the

A starving man waits for food at a United Nations feeding center in Thiet. Drought, famine, and the civil war have caused the deaths of millions of Sudanese.

world is somewhere between 700,000 and 4 million. The British-based group Anti-Slavery International believes that tens of thousands of Sudanese have been taken as slaves since 1983.

Sudan is not unique in the world for tolerating slavery. Other countries besides Sudan that have slave trafficking problems are Bahrain, Iran, Qatar, Saudi Arabia, the United Arab Emirates, Afghanistan, Armenia, Belarus, Bosnia, Cambodia, Greece, Indonesia, Kyrgyzstan, Lebanon, Myanmar, Russia, Tajikistan, and Turkey. Even in the United States, Powell said, there are about 50,000 slaves—mostly women and children working in brothels, sweatshops, farm fields, and homes against their will.

Life in Sudan comes cheap. Slaves can be purchased for as little as $15.

In recent years, there has been a new and more profitable incentive to take slaves. Some Christian organizations have been raising money to buy back slaves from their owners. These organizations are willing to pay as much as $50 to $100 per slave.

Sudanese refugees and "lost boys" huddle together at a camp inside Kenya, 1992. Between 1987 and 1993 more than 20,000 young children left their villages in Sudan and walked to refugee camps in Ethiopia and Kenya.

Despite the good intentions of such organizations, it is possible that these buybacks are doing the opposite of what they are intended to do—actually encouraging the capture of more slaves, so the slavers can be paid for their release.

In addition to slavery, Sudan's civil war has also spawned a generation of "lost boys" and "lost girls" who have been orphaned. Between 20,000 and 25,000 of these young boys fled their villages in the late 1980s, walking to Ethiopia. They returned later to Sudan and then moved on to Kenya. Since then, some of the lost boys were admitted to the U.S. One of them was John Manyok Tot, who was only five years old when he fled his home and walked 250 miles to Ethiopia with other children fleeing the war.

"A lot of people suffered," Tot recalled. "Mosquitoes, hunger, thirst. A lot of people didn't have clothes. People suffered a lot of disease. Chicken pox, diarrhea, malaria. We were walking using our bare feet. We didn't have shoes to wear." Tot was lucky that older boys took him under their wing. They carried him when he was too tired to walk and held his hand. He spent three years living in a refugee camp in Ethiopia before being sent back to Sudan and then finally ending up in Kenya in a camp without electricity, indoor plumbing, or sufficient food. Tot now lives in Pennsylvania.

While it is true that Tot and his fellow lost boys had a rough time, their lot was still better than the 2,000 to 3,000 lost Sudanese girls who never found their way to freedom. Smaller in number than their lost brothers, these girls did not get the public attention the boys did. As a result, some have been forced into slavery in the Kakkuma refugee camp in Kenya and others have been made to marry against their will for the "bride price" they bring.

EDUCATION AND THE WORKPLACE

Men dominate the workforce in Sudan with women accounting for only one-quarter of the country's workers. In the year 2000, the

"I Am Not an Animal"

Francis Bok, a young Sudanese, has become a voice against slavery in Sudan. He has traveled the United States telling audiences about the 10-year period in which he was enslaved in Sudan. St. Martin's Press has agreed to publish his story. Although the publishing house titled the book *Escape from Slavery*, Bok thinks a better title would be, "I Am Not an Animal."

Born in southern Sudan in a community of farmers, Bok was just seven years old when he was abducted on May 15, 1986. The child was heading to the market to sell his family's eggs when government soldiers on horseback began slashing their way through his village. He watched in horror as his family and male members of the tribe were killed. Women and children were abducted.

Bok was sold to a man who owned cows and wanted the boy to look after them. He made Bok sleep with the cows because, he said, Bok was an animal just like them. He was given food only once a day and had to endure beatings from his master's children. At 14, he tried to escape but was caught. His punishment, he said, was spending 10 days tied to a stake and beaten. Still, he recalled, it could have been worse. Some slave children had their legs amputated as punishment for their escape attempts.

Bok was not deterred. When he was 17 he ran away again, this time making his way to Cairo and a U.N. refugee office. He reached the United States in 1999, when he was 20 years old. At first he was not comfortable speaking publicly about his experiences as a slave. He changed his mind, he said, when he was shown photographs of other Sudanese slave children who had been maimed for life by cruel masters. "I saw those pictures of the women and children—things I had witnessed with my own eyes. I decided it would be an honor to join them and be part of what they are doing," he said. He is now an associate at the American branch of Anti-Slavery International, based in Boston.

governor of Khartoum actually banned women from working in public places.

Girls are less likely to get an education in Sudan than their brothers. Primary and secondary education is free although there are few schools in the south and not enough teachers. Few children living in the southern part of the country are able to attend school.

Less than half of the total population is able to read and write.

Fewer than 20 percent of Sudanese graduate from high school. Those who do may attend one of nine universities—if they are willing to join the militia and are devout Muslims.

Ahfad University College for Women in Omdurman is the leading women's college in Sudan with an enrollment of 4,600 students. Classes are taught mostly in English. Girls may earn undergraduate degrees in nutrition, early childhood development, office management, and pre-medicine. In 1990, the college established a school of medicine that has graduated at least 66 female doctors.

Students at Omdurman Ahlia University, which opened in 1982, can study physics and mathematics, library science, environmental studies and business administration. The school is noteworthy because it is not run by the government and is supported by private donations.

The oldest and largest of the universities is the government-run University of Khartoum. It was established in 1902 and was originally called Gordon Memorial College in honor of General Gordon. With campuses in Khartoum, Khartoum North, and Omdurman, the university has about 17,000 undergraduate and 6,000 postgraduate students enrolled. Classes at the University of Khartoum have been taught in Arabic since 1991, when President Bashir declared that all government-run universities stop their English instruction. The decree led to the resignation of 70 university instructors.

Students cannot attend the university unless they join the Popular Defense Forces, a paramilitary group associated with the National Congress Party. Once enrolled they may pursue degrees in both *Sharia* and English law as well as agriculture and veterinary sciences, engineering, computer sciences, pharmacy, nursing, architecture, and management. Its Kitchener School of Medicine, named for Lord Kitchener, Sudan's first governor general, provides the country with physicians.

Physicians are in short supply in the country, and doctors contend with drug shortages and poorly equipped medical facilities. In Sudan there is one doctor for every 6,500 people in the north and one doctor for every 83,000 people in the south. Doctors treat people for diseases often not found in the developed world—malaria, snail fever, dysentery, sleeping sickness, black fever, and measles.

Young men 18 to 33 are required to spend a minimum of 18 months in national military service. This National Service Law, passed in 1992, has led to boys and men from the southern part of the country going to war against members of their own tribes.

SPORTS IN SUDAN

If there is a national sport, it is football, a game most American children would recognize as soccer. There are pick-up games in the desert as well as organized sports clubs in Khartoum that go by the names Hilal, Mareikh, and Morada. Sudan has a national team that competes in the World Cup soccer tournaments.

Another sport that is popular is wrestling, which is practiced by many tribes, including the Nuba. In its purest form, wrestling is much more than a sport to the Nuba. It is an ancient tradition and social event that even the youngest members of the tribe participate in by trying to imitate the moves of the wrestlers who fight under such names as Camel's Leg and Four Donkeys. Every Nubian boy learns how to wrestle and dreams of being a champion. Those who are very good at it earn the right to be featured in ceremonial matches that take place after the tribe's harvest begins. The better the harvest, the more matches that will take place. Poor harvests mean that there will be no matches at all.

Wrestlers don't know when the matches will take place or who will compete until tribal elders announce the competitions. When the sun sets, messengers are dispatched to find the best wrestlers and invite them to compete. Wrestling is so popular that the populations of entire villages may turn out for them, perhaps walking as far as 20 miles to get there. Their champion will carry with him the flag that represents their community. The flag is usually kept in a special house with other accoutrements used in the sport—drums, a long horn, and the clothing the wrestlers will wear.

The villagers march to the competition with their champion at the front. Before the matches start the wrestlers form a circle and crouch as ashes are scattered over them. A communal prayer is offered for their champion to prevail.

Less skilled wrestlers usually go first. Sometimes more than one match goes on at the same time as the men try to knock their opponent on his back to win the match. A match is a draw if the two men are equally strong and unable to distinguish themselves.

Some Sudanese wrestling matches are broadcast on satellite television. In Omdurman it is also possible to see Nuba wrestling. The Nubas used to wrestle for fun, glory, and tradition. Now some are doing it for trophies and money.

MUSEUMS AND ENTERTAINMENT

Many of the country's most popular entertainers went into exile after the Bashir government limited their ability to perform. One such performer, 70-year-old Mohamed Wardi, recently attracted tens of thousands of fans to the airport when he returned to the Sudan after spending 13 years in self-imposed exile in Egypt. Wardi had left Sudan just a few months after President Bashir took over. Wardi is well known for his leftist politics and romantic and patriotic songs about the Nile and everyday life in the country. He sings in Arabic and in his native Nubian dialect.

Sudan's museums celebrate the country's history. The best known are the National Museum in Khartoum and the Khalifa House Museum in Omdurman.

The National Museum is home to archeological artifacts

representing every era of Sudanese civilization. An outdoor garden features reconstructed monuments and temples that were rescued from being flooded when the Egyptians built the Aswan Dam. Inside the museum proper are artifacts from the early Paleolithic period through the coming of Islam. The museum has been open since 1971.

The Khalifa House Museum is a good place to see artifacts from the Mahdi period in Sudan. The oldest part of the museum was built in 1888 and was occupied by the Mahdi's successor, Khalifa Abdullah Ben Mohamed. The museum has many everyday objects once used by the Khalifa on display.

A TRADITIONAL MEAL

The people of Sudan are often glad to share their homes and food with their guests. If one were lucky enough to be invited for dinner, first would come an offer of a refreshing fruit drink called *abre* or *tabrihana*. A sheep might be slaughtered in the visitors' honor.

The guests and family would sit on cushions placed on the floor surrounding a plain, low table. Before eating, everyone would wash their hands at the table using water from a pitcher. After drying their hands with a towel, they would each receive a large cloth to put in their laps to keep their clothing clean. Most foods would be eaten with the right hand.

The first course might be lentil soup or *shorba*, a lamb-based broth fragrant with peanut butter and lemon, served in individual bowls. Next there would be five or six dishes that would be eaten by hand using a flat bread like *kisra*, which resembles a pancake and is made from a grain called **durra**. These dishes could include *maschi* (a tomato dish stuffed with ground beef), *koftah* (ground meatballs), and *salatet zabady bil ajur* (a mixture of plain yogurt, garlic, cucumber, and salt). A spicy condiment called *shata* is also placed on the table for diners to mix with their food.

Sudanese people in ceremonial costume participate in a traditional wedding dance.

It would be rare to find pork or alcohol at a Sudanese meal, as these are forbidden by Islamic law. (The punishment for those caught eating pork or drinking alcohol is 40 lashes with a whip.)

Meals are usually eaten without a beverage, but after dinner a special coffee called *guhwah* will be served. Sudanese coffee is unlike coffee available in America. Coffee beans are fried over charcoal in a pot called a *jebena*. The fried coffee beans are next ground with cloves and spices and steeped in boiling water. The coffee is strained through a sieve and served in small coffee cups. Non-coffee drinkers might have *kakaday*, hibiscus tea served Sudanese style with plenty of sugar, or *laban*, sweet milk that can be served hot or cold. While the diners drink their steamy beverages, the host may light an incense burner that suffuses the room with a pleasant scent.

The meal is often finished with small slices of peeled fruit, as well as a sweet such as creme caramela, a caramel flavored pudding, or *zabadi*, a honey sweetened yogurt.

Escape from Sudan

At 7 feet, 7 inches tall and wearing size 15-1/2 sneakers, Manute Bol was like no player American basketball fans had ever seen when he stepped onto the court as a member of the Washington Bullets in 1985. In his rookie year, the slender young man from Sudan set an NBA record for the number of blocked shots in one game. Blocking shots was easy for Bol, the tallest man to ever play in the NBA.

During the 11 years he played professional basketball in America, the "Dinka Dunker" became rich, earning more than $1.5 million a season. Ironically, as his fortunes rose, those of his people in the National Republic of the Sudan continued to fall.

Bol was the son of a Dinka tribal leader in the village of Turalie, located in the Sudd swampland. His nomadic kinsmen have been among the hardest hit by the years of civil war in Sudan. His childhood village, Turalie, has been wiped out.

When his basketball career ended in 1996, Manute Bol moved to Uganda so that he could be close to Sudan if peace ever came to the troubled country. A year later, the rebel factions signed a peace treaty, and Bol was invited to return to Sudan to help the country rebuild. Sadly, the peace did not last. Soon after Bol returned, warfare broke out again.

Bol soon found himself the victim of prejudice. As a black Christian living in Khartoum, Bol was made to feel unwelcome by the ruling Islamic majority. He was told he could not have a job until he converted to Islam. This he refused to do.

There were other hardships. His 11-year pro basketball career had taken a terrible toll on his body, and Bol developed arthritis. But even though the aches in his joints were quite painful, Bol resisted the idea of visiting a doctor in Khartoum. The reason? All the doctors are Muslims, and Bol feared that as a southern Sudanese he would be poisoned in the doctor's office.

"They'll kill you," he said. "Doctors are fundamentalist people. They shoot you with medicine you don't know. Or maybe they drop something in your tea. When I go to their house I don't drink tea. I don't drink soda. That's the only way I survive because a lot of people were killed like that."

Finally, he decided to leave Sudan. When he was unable to obtain a passport from the Sudanese government, in 2001 he bribed some government officials and escaped to Egypt along with his wife and child. From Egypt, Bol eventually emigrated to the United States.

Bol returned to the United States in March 2002 virtually penniless. Much of the money he had earned playing basketball had been spent on trying to improve the welfare of the Sudanese; Bol also gave about $3.5 million to the Sudan People's Liberation Movement. "When you find that your people are living in a bad situation then you have to help your people. We thought that we had been forgotten by the world," Bol said.

Bol has established a fund to help the people of Sudan and has raised money for this charity in various ways. In May 2002 he accepted $30,000 to appear in a clownish celebrity boxing match on national television. His opponent was William "Refrigerator" Perry, a former professional football player. Bol won the match and donated his purse to the relief fund. And in the fall of 2002 he signed a contract with a minor-league hockey team, again donating much of the money he earned to the fund.

Kabashiya, a small town on the Nile River, is typical of many towns in Sudan. The buildings are constructed of mud bricks.

Communities

The best known and most populous city in Sudan is Khartoum, which in Arabic means "elephant trunk," a shape the city resembles from the above. The city, and its nearby sister cities of Khartoum North (also known as Bahri) and Omdurman, contains about 5 million residents. The "three sisters" are connected to one another by bridges.

As the capital of Sudan, Khartoum is home to embassies and other government-related offices. Most of the country's businesses are headquartered there along with most of the country's doctors. It has been the capital since 1834.

Located where the Blue Nile and White Nile come together, Khartoum was a natural place for people to settle. But it owes its existence as a city to Muhammad Ali's son, Ismail, who chose it for his military outpost. Khartoum served as a center for the slave trade in Sudan; its location made it a convenient place for slavers to launch raiding parties in the south to pick up slaves they could sell to Egyptians and Turks.

It was in Khartoum that the Mahdi and General Gordon had their showdown. The place where Gordon fell, now called the People's Palace, is where President Bashir lives today.

After Gordon's death the stunned Englishmen returned more than a decade later to take their revenge at the battle of Omdurman. When the victorious English rebuilt Khartoum, they laid the streets out in the shape of their own Union Jack flag. Thousands of workmen toiled to build beautiful buildings along the river and plant hundreds of shade trees. The English also created North Khartoum across the Blue Nile from the older city to house industry. There, one can find dockyards, meat packing plants, textile weaving enterprises, rubber plants, concrete manufacturing and shoe manufacturers. North Khartoum contains some of the most expensive houses in the area while in nearby Omdurman, mud-walled houses are typical abodes for city workers.

Glimmers of Khartoum's past colonial elegance can still be seen today in the aging city. Thousands of young Sudanese orphans fend for themselves in the streets of Khartoum while an estimated 1.5 million southern Sudanese have been relocated to refuge camps near the city.

Despite being the country's capital, Khartoum is not a big tourist destination. It has only 11 hotels. Only recently has the city's telephone system become reliable. There is one television station in the entire country and few radio stations. Before Bashir took over the country had 55 newspapers and magazines, 22 of which were published in Khartoum. The government banned those newspapers and arrested some journalists when Bashir first took over. Now the country has only a few government-controlled papers.

From midnight to 5 A.M. in Khartoum, people on the streets are subject to questioning by the police. Foreigners may be asked to show their passports. Furthermore, no photographs can be taken within the city without a permit and photographs of military areas, bridges, public utilities, broadcasting stations and street people are never allowed.

> **Visitors are rare in Sudan and easily attract crowds the way a celebrity would in America. The word for foreigners in Arabic is *khawajas*.**

Banyan and mahogany trees line the streets of Khartoum. Most of the homes are simple, one-story structures.

Where the Nile rivers come together there is a park-like area in which flowers bloom and many different types of birds gather.

There are few private automobiles in Khartoum—or anywhere else in the country, for that matter. The Sudanese drive on the left side of the road and because there are shortages of parts and mechanics, their cars frequently break down and are abandoned. More commonly, people take buses or trucks more suitable for cargo than human beings.

Glass and textile manufacturing, printing and food processing are the major industries found in Khartoum.

OMDURMAN

About 526,000 people live in Omdurman, which lacks the sophistication of Khartoum despite the fact that it was at one time the capital of Sudan. Roads are unpaved and there is no commercial center. It boasts the biggest marketplace in Sudan, the Suk el-Kebir. For 1,800 years peddlers and craftsman have lined its narrow streets, jostling for customers to sell their wares. At the *souk* one can purchase fish, vegetables, and fruit as well as candlesticks, leather goods made from snakeskin and crocodile, gold and silver jewelry, and goods made from ivory.

Located near the *souk* is a more specialized marketplace, an unusual attraction called the Mowelih. This is Omdurman's Camel

Market, just the place to purchase a one-humped Arabian beast made for desert travel. From their nostrils, which close up during dust storms, to the location of their ears which also keeps the sand at bay, camels are perfect desert creatures. More sand protection is achieved through the tough pads on their knees and chests. Camels are notoriously unfussy when it comes to food, making a meal out of the scrubby vegetation that grows where nothing else will. Their fat-filled humps make it possible for them to go without food and water for long periods of time.

Twice a week new camels are brought to the Mowelih from western Sudan where they will be purchased by buyers who desire them as investments or basic transportation. The Mowelih takes up one square mile of the Sahara and most of the camels that are purchased there will end up in Libya or Egypt. While the camels get the once over from prospective buyers, they are immobilized by having their left front leg tied in a bent position.

Omdurman is home to the Mahdi's tomb and to the Khalifa's House Museum. The original Mahdi's tomb was destroyed by Lord Kitchener but because of the tomb's emotional significance, it was rebuilt in 1947.

Omdurman is famous for its "whirling dervishes," religious Muslims who dance themselves into a frenzy every Friday on Islam's holy day. Dressed in white from their turbans to their *jalabiyyas*, these men gather in front of the tomb of Sheikh Hamed al-Nil on the western side of Omdurman. Nil was a 19th century holy man who drowned, yet when his body turned up two months after his demise, it had not decayed. Nil is thought to be capable of carrying out miracles today.

The dervishes and other holy men form a circle and, to the beat of drums and chants, whirl around in dizzying fashion to become closer to God.

PORT SUDAN

Port Sudan, the country's only seaport, is located on the Red Sea about 800 miles northeast of Khartoum. It is through Port Sudan that the Sudanese trade their goods with the rest of the world. The city was established by the British in 1905; today it is home to about a million people, including refugees from Chad, Uganda, Eritrea, and Ethiopia. Pilgrims on the way to Mecca in Saudi Arabia often pass through the city.

While Port Sudan is not the thriving terminal it once was there are signs that its fortunes may be improving. An international chain recently built a luxury hotel in the city. Also encouraging was the news that Ethiopia, which has no seaport of its own, has agreed to use Port Sudan for its shipping needs. Most importantly, a pipeline completed in 1999 brings oil from Sudan's oil fields to tankers anchored at the port.

CELEBRATIONS IN SUDAN

As one might expect, a country beset by civil war and poverty and run by a dictator is not given to extravagant celebrations. Sudan has few national holidays. Its biggest is Independence Day. Every year

Muslim women shop in Omdurman, which is home to the largest marketplace in Sudan, the Suk el-Kebir. Unlike many villages in southern Sudan, Omdurman has many modern conveniences.

Waratit, a Dinka village, is made up of grass huts. People here live in much the same way as their ancestors did hundreds of years ago.

on January 1, the Sudanese people celebrate their liberation from the Egyptian and British Condominium Government. Parades of soldiers march through the streets of Khartoum to mark the occasion.

Another holiday celebrated in the country is Unity Day, on March 27. This commemorates the signing of the Addis Ababa agreement in 1972. The agreement ended the civil war for a time and gave hope that peace would last. It did not.

Weddings are important celebrations in Khartoum. Girls often get married at age 15 or 16. Friends, family members, and neighbors are invited to wedding ceremonies, which can last into the wee hours of the morning. The bride is often attired in a white dress and veil and adorned with gold coins on her bodice, gold rings on her fingers, and gold jewelry on her wrists. In a traditional service bride and groom sit outside under a canopy as their guests greet them.

The bridal pair does not say a word as the guests file by. Hours may pass. Then the bride and her mother disappear and later, the bride returns wearing a different dress capped by a golden crown linked by a chain to her nose. The bride then begins a sensual dance for her groom to the rhythm laid down by a drummer. She dances for a while then stops and is cheered by the crowd. Then she starts again, sometimes presenting as many as 30 different short dances for her groom. When her dancing is done, her guests dance around her. To show their approval of her performance they click their fingers—the Sudanese equivalent of applause—before they leave the young couple to start their new life.

Other holidays popularly celebrated by the Sudanese are those that are important to its national religion, Islam. For example, many Sudanese celebrate the birthday of Muhammad, who was born in Mecca in 570. Children especially enjoy this holiday because of the sweets they receive and the presence of street entertainers. And like other Muslims, Islamic Sudanese fast during daylight hours in the month of Ramadan and at the end of the month take part in a three-day holiday called Eid al-Fitr, which marks the end of Ramadan. (The Arabic word *eid* means "holiday.")

There is also a four-day holiday called Eid al-Adha, which commemorates the willingness of the patriarch Abraham to sacrifice his son when asked to do so by Allah. According to the Qur'an, God prevents Abraham from sacrificing his son by having a ram take the boy's place. The Eid al-Adha celebration involves slaughtering a sheep, cow, or goat and making it the centerpiece of a meal that will be shared by friends, neighbors, family, and the poor people of the community. Two-thirds of the meal is supposed to be given away as charity. Eid al-Adha is celebrated during the last month of the Islamic calendar.

An angry crowd gestures and waves pictures of Osama bin Laden during a protest in Khartoum against military strikes on Afghanistan, October 2001. Sudan harbored the terrorist leader from 1991 to 1996, but its government agreed to work with the United States in its war on terrorism after the September 11, 2001, attacks by members of bin Laden's al-Qaeda terrorist network.

Foreign Relations

usk was just settling over Khartoum on August 20, 1998, when dozens of cruise missiles, launched from U.S. ships on the Red Sea, struck and obliterated their target. The al-Shifa pharmaceutical plant, only a year old and one of the most modern structures in Sudan, was now little more than a flaming pile of rubble.

At the same time al-Shifa was being hammered, the U.S. also struck terrorist camps in Afghanistan. The two-pronged attack ordered by U.S. President Bill Clinton was meant to send a message to countries harboring terrorists. Sudan is such a country.

Although Sudan has agreed to support international conventions to end terrorism, the country remains on a U.S. list of countries that sponsor terrorism, along with Cuba, Iran, Iraq, Libya, North Korea, and Syria.

A HAVEN FOR TERRORISTS

Sudanese law allows any Muslim to enter the country without a visa. Under that law, in 1991 the Saudi Arabian–born terrorist leader Osama bin Laden was allowed into the country, where he set up training camps for his Afghan resistance fighters known as *mujahideen*. Bin Laden, a member of a wealthy Saudi Arabian family that had made a fortune in the construction business, brought hundreds of Afghan *mujahideen* with him and used his considerable wealth to create new businesses in Sudan. By some estimates he brought as much as $350 million with him to Sudan. He became a hero to many Sudanese Muslims when he used his family's construction equipment to build a long awaited 500-mile highway from Khartoum to Port Sudan on the Red Sea coast. His construction companies also built a new airport in Port Sudan, and bin Laden donated $2.5 million toward its operation.

Bin Laden remained in Sudan until 1996, when Bashir's government expelled him under pressure from the United States. Even after bin Laden left, however, Sudan remained under suspicion by Western powers. The U.S. government believed the al-Shifa pharmaceutical plant was linked to bin Laden's al-Qaeda terrorist organization and was used to manufactured chemical weapons, even though Sudan's government denied this link and the plant's owner, Saleh Idris, claimed he had never met bin Laden.

The U.S. never proved that chemical weapons were made at the al-Shifa facility. In fact, the public nature of the plant made it an unlikely site for a secret weapons program. After opening in 1997, the plant had been opened for tours by many visitors, both Sudanese and international: foreign ministers and ambassadors representing other countries, World Health Organization personnel, and even school children.

The 1998 attack on the al-Shifa pharmaceutical plant came two weeks after terrorists exploded truck bombs at American embassies in Nairobi, Kenya, and Dar es Salaam, Tanzania. The August 7, 1998, embassy attacks left over 200 people dead and more than 5,000 injured. In authorizing the attacks, President Bill Clinton said, "Our target was terror. Our mission was to strike at the network of radical groups affiliated with and funded by Osama bin Laden, perhaps the biggest organizer and financier of international terrorism in the world today." In May 2001, four men were convicted in absentia for their roles in the embassy bombings. All four are believed to have been members of al-Qaeda.

(Left, inset) An American honor guard accompanies the remains of a victim of the 1998 U.S. embassy bombing in Nairobi, Kenya, during a ceremony at Andrews Air Force Base, Maryland. The August 7, 1998, attacks on the embassies in Kenya and Tanzania killed at least 252 people (including 12 Americans) and injured more than 5,000. U.S. Secretary of State Madeleine Albright promised to "use all means at our disposal to track down and punish" those responsible. (Right) U.S. Secretary of Defense William S. Cohen (left) and General Henry H. Shelton, the chairman of the Joint Chiefs of Staff, brief reporters about the retaliatory strike on the al-Shifa plant in Sudan and terrorist training camps in Afghanistan on August 20, 1998.

Osama bin Laden is not the only well-known terrorist to have sought sanctuary in Sudan. Ilich Ramirez Sanchez, better known as "Carlos the Jackal," was discovered living under an assumed name in Sudan in 1994. The Venezuelan-born "terrorist for hire" is considered one of the 20th century's most notorious criminals. His exploits include masterminding an invasion of an Organization of Petroleum Exporting Countries (OPEC) conference in Vienna and taking 81 hostages. Carlos the Jackal and the hostages were given safe passage to Algiers and he walked away with $50 million in ransom money.

While Carlos was a fugitive, he was found guilty in absentia of the murders of two French intelligence agents. The Paris court sentenced him to life in prison.

The Sudanese turned Carlos over to the French authorities on August 14, 1994, after they were alerted to the fact that he was in

This grainy photo of Ilich Ramirez Sanchez was one of the few pictures international law-enforcement authorities had to help them track the infamous terrorist. Nicknamed Carlos the Jackal, he was one of the most dangerous terrorists of the 1970s and 1980s. A revolutionary for hire, his employers are believed to have included Libya's Mu'ammar Muhammad al-Gadhafi, Iraq's Saddam Hussein, Syria's Hafez Assad, Cuba's Fidel Castro, and the Popular Front for the Liberation of Palestine (PFLP). Carlos disappeared in the late 1980s; he was arrested by Sudanese police in 1994 and turned over to France, where he had previously been convicted of killing two French intelligence agents.

their country. He might still be living in Sudan, however, had it not been for his lifestyle, which was not in line with the behavior expected of a practicing Muslim. Carlos openly visited nightclubs, drinking and partying with women.

When French authorities traced Carlos to Sudan, Bashir's government was not anxious to turn him over to them. The terrorist was in the country as a guest of Hassan al-Turabi, at that time head of the National Islamic Front and one of the most influential men in Sudan. Turabi relented, however, when he was shown a secretly taped video of Carlos' over-the-top behavior at a party.

Another terrorist, the blind Egyptian Sheikh Umar Abd ar-Rahman, was officially welcomed into Sudan by the fundamentalist government despite his comprehensive résumé of destruction. Rahman may have been involved in the 1981 assassination of Egyptian president Anwar Sadat; he was definitely involved in the 1993 terrorist attack on the World Trade Center in New York City, as well as a 1995 plot to kill Sadat's successor, Hosni Mubarak, and other American and U.N. leaders.

In 1990 Rahman entered the United States using a visa he had received from Khartoum; he planned terrorist operations from a base in New Jersey. Sheikh Rahman was arrested in 1994 along with a number of his co-conspirators (many of them Sudanese, including his lieutenant Siddiq Ibrahim Siddiq 'Ali). The sheikh was tried, found guilty, and sentenced to life imprisonment.

Through the 1990s, Sudan provided military training and support to a number of terrorist organizations, including Hezbollah (a Shiite Muslim group in Lebanon) and Hamas (a militant Palestinian organization). These groups are opposed to the existence of Israel as a state. In 2002, the president of Sudan called on Muslims throughout the world to support the Palestinians in their violent struggle against Israel. Sudan has also supported terrorist groups that operate in Egypt, Algeria, Ethiopia, Eritrea, Uganda, and Tunisia.

SUDAN AND THE UNITED STATES

In recent decades, the foreign policies of Sudan and the United States have been at opposite ends of the spectrum. In addition to Sudan's support of terrorists, it has also supported regimes in Iran, Iraq, and Libya that have been strongly opposed by the U.S. at times in the 1980s and 1990s.

In the fall of 1990, for example, when the U.S. was building a coalition of nations to act against Iraq, which had invaded and annexed neighboring Kuwait, it asked Sudan to join. The Sudanese government decided instead to support Iraqi strongman Saddam Hussein, and refused to allow the coalition to operate from bases in Sudan. After the Gulf War, Sudan's willingness to align with Iraq isolated it further from both the United States and from Arab countries like Saudi Arabia.

The U.S. broke off diplomatic relations with Sudan in 1996, after Sudan was linked to an unsuccessful attempt to assassinate Egyptian President Hosni Mubarak in Addis Ababa, Ethiopia. The U.S. closed its embassy in Khartoum, and both the United States and the United Nations imposed economic sanctions against Sudan.

Sudan was prepared for retaliation from the United States after September 11, 2001, when the World Trade Center in New York City was destroyed by terrorists trained by bin Laden's al-Qaeda organization. Anticipating an attack, the government of Sudan shut down the Giad industrial complex, a large manufacturing plant located 30 miles from Khartoum. (Ironically, this complex is owned by Salad Idris, the man who had also owned the al-Shifa plant.) But this time the U.S. did not attack Sudan. What had changed was that Sudan had pledged to cooperate with the U.S. in its war on terrorism.

Sudan had earlier agreed to support two international agreements to end terrorism—the 1997 International Convention for the Suppression of Terrorist Bombings and the 1999 International

Former U.S. Senator John Danforth (center) is presented as special envoy to Sudan by President George W. Bush (right) and Secretary of State Colin Powell on September 6, 2001, outside the White House. In the summer of 2002 Danforth met with Sudanese officials after an accord was signed between the government and the SPLA.

Convention for the Suppression of the Financing of Terrorism. After the September 11 attacks, Sudan gave the U.S. government information it had on suspected al-Qaeda members. In March 2002 the Sudanese arrested and turned over to the U.S. a suspected al-Qaeda leader, Abu Anas al-Liby, who is considered one of the most dangerous terrorists in the world. Al-Liby is believed to have helped plan the African embassy bombings. In addition, the Sudanese government arrested many other non-Sudanese Muslim fundamentalists within the country.

Even before Sudan's cooperation in the war on terrorism, President George W. Bush had taken more of an interest in improving U.S.-Sudan relations. He showed that interest by appointing former Senator John Danforth as special envoy for peace in Sudan. Danforth's delegation to Sudan was accorded great respect and given free rein to visit areas normally off-limits to outsiders—particularly southern Sudan and the Nuba Mountains. Danforth was instrumental in arranging a Nuba Mountain cease-fire that allowed humanitarian aid to be delivered safely to the hard-hit region. International agencies are helping to monitor the cease-fire.

America has also decided to support a Kenyan-led effort to broker peace in the Sudan called the Intergovernmental Authority for Development (IGAD). This conflict resolution organization is composed of representatives from Sudan, Ethiopia, Djibouti, Uganda, and Eritrea.

Despite this recent warming in the relationship between the United States and Sudan, the country remains on the U.S. list of countries that sponsor terrorism. In October 2001, when the U.N. Security Council lifted the sanctions imposed on Sudan after the

Sudanese police arrested Abu Anas al-Liby in early 2002, while rounding up suspected al-Qaeda members in the country. The FBI considered the Libyan terrorist leader one of the 22 most dangerous terrorists in the world; he is thought to be Osama bin Laden's computer expert. Sudan handed al-Liby over to U.S. authorities in March 2002.

1995 Mubarak assassination attempt, one country abstained from the vote—the United States.

SUDAN AND ITS AFRICAN NEIGHBORS

In addition to improved relations with the United States, Sudan has been making friendly overtures to its neighbors. Sudan and Ethiopia, for example, have reached agreements to buy and sell electricity, link their countries by railroad, and build an oil pipeline.

Mu'ammar Muhammad al-Gadhafi, the head of state in Libya, has helped Sudan and Uganda develop closer ties. The governments of these two countries had been working at cross purposes by supporting each other's rebel factions. Now, Uganda has vowed to end its support of the SPLA while Sudan has promised to offer no assistance to Uganda's Lord's Resistance Army. President Bashir attended the inauguration of Uganda's new president, Yoweri Museveni.

Of course, Sudan and Uganda have made similar agreements before that both have violated. The security of their 270-mile (435-km) common border has been difficult for both countries to maintain. Rebels, smugglers, and other undesirables have historically had little trouble moving from one country to another and the two countries' efforts to destabilize each other displaced thousands of Sudanese to Uganda and thousands of Ugandans to Sudan. In the process, both countries have squandered money and civilian lives and laid waste to many villages and towns.

Sudan recently ended a decade of rocky relations with Tunisia when that country sent its foreign minister, Mustapha Othman Ismail, to Sudan for a visit. Ismail's visit was the first made by a Tunisian government official in ten years. Tunisia had split with Sudan over its support for an Islamic fundamentalist movement called En-Nahda. The movement no longer exists.

SUDAN AND EGYPT

The failed 1995 Mubarak assassination attempt severely strained ties between the neighboring countries. Ten bullets were fired at Mubarak's limousine as he traveled through the Ethiopian city of Addis Ababa; none struck their intended target. The house from which the gunmen had coordinated the attack had been rented by Sudanese citizens and the assassins had entered Ethiopia from Sudan. With Mubarak gone, Sudanese leaders apparently hoped Egypt would establish an Islamic government.

While the Egyptians did not break diplomatic relations over the assassination attempt, some fighting did occur days later at the border between the two countries. Egypt sent Sudan's nationals home and Sudan did the same with Egypt's nationals. President Mubarak publicly accused the Sudan government of plotting his death and, for the first time, came out in support of the Sudan's southern rebels.

Nevertheless the two countries remain inextricably linked by their connection to the Nile River. More than ever, Egyptians need the Nile's water to survive now that its population has more than doubled in the past 20 years. Water conservation projects, which could benefit both countries, have been delayed as the Sudan continues to use most of its economic resources to carry on its civil war.

One of the main areas of tension between Egypt and Sudan has been the "soft" border between the two countries, called the Halayib Triangle. The condominium agreement between Egypt and Britain, signed in 1899, established Sudan's border with Egypt at 22 degrees north latitude. That placed the Halayib Triangle, an area of 15,625 square miles, in Egypt. There was, however, a problem with this artificial border. It arbitrarily split several tribes in half, separating them by the new border. To correct that wrong and allow the tribes to cross the border as they pleased, Egypt agreed to let Sudan administer the Halayib Triangle in 1902. Still, Egypt did not renounce its claim to the region.

This arrangement worked fine until Sudan became an independent nation in 1956. The triangle then became the focus of a standoff when both countries brought their armies to the border. The pressure cooled when Egypt realized that Sudan was willing to go to war with Egypt over the disputed area and decided to back down. Egyptian President Gamal Abdel Nasser told the Sudanese, "Take Halayib and take Aswan, if you desire. I shall not allow Arab

Refugees leave Sudan and return to their homes in Eritrea, June 2000. Some 20,000 refugees had been forced to leave their home, the Eritrean town of Tesseney, after Ethiopian forces captured the town. Many moved across the border to Sudan, where they lived in camps under difficult conditions for about two weeks, until the town was recaptured.

blood to be shed on the lands of Egypt or the Sudan, however grave the issue."

For the next two decades, Halayib ceased to be an issue. It remained an Egyptian territory administered by the government of Sudan. Problems developed again when the government decided to open the area for oil exploration. Without consulting Egypt, in 1978 Sudan granted a U.S. company the right to search for oil in the area. When Cairo discovered this breach, the Egyptian government agreed to the oil exploration—as long as Egypt received a fair share of the revenues. The U.S. oil company abandoned the project in 1983, after it was unable to find sufficient quantities of oil and natural gas.

Hostilities flared anew when Sudan once again offered the rights to explore in the region to a Canadian oil company without consulting the Egyptians. At the same time Sudan stopped an Egyptian company from extracting magnesium in the triangle, even though it had been operating in the area for three-quarters of a century, and requested that Egyptians living in the triangle carry Sudanese identity cards.

Hosni Mubarak (left), the president of Egypt, walks with Sudan's president, Omar al-Bashir, during a meeting in Cairo in December 1999. Relations between the neighboring countries have been strained, particularly in the aftermath of a failed 1995 attempt by Sudanese terrorists to assassinate Mubarak in Addis Ababa, Ethiophia.

By 2002, the issue of the Halayib Triangle had simmered down again. Egypt and the Sudan have signed some commercial agreements and neither country wants to go to war over the area.

THE FUTURE OF SUDAN

As Sudan attempts to improve its standing in the world community by cooperating in the fight against terrorism and working with its neighbors, its future as a unified country remains uncertain. In October 2002, the Sudanese government and the southern rebels agreed to a cease-fire, during which time the two sides would resume peace talks in Machakos, Kenya, aimed at ending the long civil war.

One possible resolution that was discussed in Kenya would give the Christian and animist people of the south six years of self-rule. After that, a referendum vote would allow the people of the region to decide whether to remain part of Sudan, or break away and form a separate country.

It remains to be seen whether Sudan will remain a Muslim state dominated by a military dictatorship, or if the renewed efforts of the United States and other western nations to bring peace to the troubled country can help the growth of freedom and democracy in Sudan.

circa 2000 B.C.: The early civilization of Cush, located along the Nile River, trades with Egypt.

circa 1,500 B.C.: Cush becomes a province of Egypt under the rule of Pharaoh Ahmose I.

750 B.C.: The Cushite king Kashta conquers portions of Egypt.

Circa 600 B.C.: Merotic civilization begins to rise along the Nile.

24 B.C.: Angered by Merotic incursions into Roman-controlled Egypt, Roman legions invade Meroe and bring the region under the control of the empire.

a.d. 350: The Auxmites destroy Meroe.

circa 570: Muhammad, whose teaching will become the basis of Islam, is born; three kingdoms in the Sudan region (Nobatia, Muqurra, and Alwa) are converted to Christianity.

700: Nobatia and Muqurra merge to form the kingdom of Dunqulah, which resists the advance of Islam until the 13th century.

1276: The Mamluk rulers of Egypt gain power over Dunqulah.

1315: The first Muslim king takes the throne in Dunqulah.

1517: The Ottoman Turks absorb Egypt and Dunqulah into their empire.

1820: The Egyptian warlord Muhammad Ali sends a force to invade Sudan; the region soon comes under Egypt's control.

1869: The Suez Canal opens.

1882: Great Britain becomes involved in Egyptian and Sudanese affairs.

1883: The Mahdi declares *jihad* against the foreign rule of the Sudan.

1885: Khartoum destroyed by the Mahdi, who makes Omdurman his capital.

1898: The forces of the Khalifa are defeated by British troops under Lord Kitchener.

1899: The condominium period of joint rule by Great Britain and Egypt begins in Sudan; it will last until 1955.

1902: The first college (eventually called the University of Khartoum) is established in Sudan; Egypt agrees to let Sudan administer the disputed Halayib Triangle area.

1956: Sudan becomes an independent country.

CHRONOLOGY

1958: Civilian government is elected, then quickly overthrown by military coup.

1962: Civil war begins between the Islamic north and Christian south.

1964: Sudanese students, civil servants, and trade unionists protest the Abbud government; riots break out in Khartoum and other cities.

1965: New elections are held, and a coalition government led by Muhammad Ahmed Mahjub is elected.

1966: Mahjub is forced to step down, and Sadiq al-Mahdi takes power.

1967: Mahdi coalition government collapses, and Mahjub returns to power as prime minister.

1969: Jaafar al-Nimeri takes over the government.

1972: Southern Sudan becomes autonomous under the Addis Ababa agreement, and much of the fighting ends.

1973: Sudan's first constitution is adopted.

1978: Oil is discovered in Sudan.

1983: President Nimeri declares *Sharia* to be the law of Sudan, and the civil war resumes after a ten-year break.

1985: Coup against Nimeri leaves military government in charge.

1986: Sadiq al-Mahdi forms coalition government.

1989: Military coup planned by Hassan al-Turabi, leader of the National Islamic Front, and carried out by General Omar al-Bashir, overturns al-Mahdi's government; Bashir installs martial law in the country.

1991: Terrorist leader Osama bin Laden enters Sudan.

1993: Bashir is elected president of Sudan.

1995: An attempt to assassinate Egyptian President Hosni Mubarak, in which a number of Sudanese nationals are involved, fails.

1996: Sudan expels terrorist leader Osama bin Laden.

1998: The United States destroys a pharmaceutical factory suspected of making chemical weapons in Khartoum.

1999: Sudan's National Assembly is disbanded; oil exports begin with the completion of a pipeline from the oil fields in the south to Port Sudan.

2000: President Bashir re-elected to a second five-year term with 86 percent of the vote in an election widely condemned as rigged.

CHRONOLOGY

2001: U.N. Security Council lifts travel sanctions against Sudan; former U.S. Senator John Danforth is named special envoy to Sudan; Hassan al-Turabi is arrested for treason after signing agreement with the SPLA.

2002: The government at Khartoum and the SPLA hold talks to discuss ending the civil war.

2003: The members of the Arab League meet in Bahrain.

GLOSSARY

Anglo-Egyptian—relating to the links that exist between Great Britain and Egypt.

animist—someone who believes that things in nature (for example, trees, mountains, and the sky) have souls or consciousness.

Byzantine Empire—The eastern branch of the Roman Empire, which broke away in A.D. 330 and survived the fall of the Roman Empire in the fifth century. The Byzantine Empire was based in modern-day Turkey and at one time controlled much of the eastern Mediterranean region. It lasted until 1453, when Constantinople, the Byzantine capital, was captured by the Ottoman Turks.

cataract—a series of river rapids and small waterfalls.

condominium—a system under which a country is ruled by two or more other nations.

coup—the sudden overthrow of a government, especially by the military.

dervish—a follower of a Muslim whose style of worship includes using physical movement to enter a trance like state.

dowry—an amount of money or property given by a bride's family to her groom when they marry.

durra—a grain grown for food and animal feed in tropical or arid areas.

fundamentalist—someone who participates in a religious movement based on a literal interpretation of religious doctrine and strict adherence to that doctrine.

Funj—one of the most powerful African people of eastern Sudan from the 15th to the 19th centuries. They ruled the Kingdom of Sennar until 1821, when an Egyptian invasion ended their dominance.

hors de combat—out of action; a military term meaning too injured to fight.

howitzer—a short cannon that fires projectiles with relatively high trajectories.

humanitarian aid—money, food, and other things given with the intention of improving the lives of other people.

indigenous—native to a particular region.

inflation—an increase in the supply of money and credit relative to available goods and services, resulting in a continuing rise in the general price level.

Islamist—radical, militant, or extremist Muslim beliefs.

junta—a group of military officers who have taken control of a country following a coup d'état.

Mamluk—former slaves who eventually became the rulers of Egypt, holding power from A.D. 1250 to 1517.

martial law—law administered by military forces during a period of war, unrest, or another emergency during which the civilian government may be unable to maintain order.

Maxim—an early type of machine gun named for its inventor, Hiram Maxim. First used by the British Army in 1891, the Maxim gun was capable of firing 650 rounds of ammunition a minute.

millet—a fast-growing cereal plant used for food in Africa.

pantheon—all the deities of a particular religion considered collectively.

referendum—a vote by the entire electorate on a specific question put to it by a government or similar body.

relief—a type of sculpture in which the design projects slightly from a flat background.

savanna—a flat grassland in a tropical or subtropical region.

sorghum—a tall cereal grass cultivated in tropical areas as a grain crop and for animal feed.

Sufism—a mystical form of Islam.

FURTHER READING

Bombay, Carl. R. *Let My People Go: The True Story of Present-Day Persecution and Slavery*. Oregon: Multnomah Publishing, 1998.

Churchill, Winston. *The River War: An Account of the Reconquest of the Sudan*. New York: Carroll & Graf, 2000.

Daley, M. W., and P. M. Holt. *A History of the Sudan from the Coming of Islam to the Present Day*. Boston: Addison-Wesley, 2000.

Featherstone, Donald. *Omdurman 1898: Kitchener's Victory in the Sudan.* Oxford, United Kingdom: Osprey Publishing, 1998.

Franck, Irene M., and David M. Brownstone. *Trade and Travel Routes Across Africa and Arabia*. New York: Facts on File, 1991.

Levy, Patricia Marjory. *Sudan*. New York: Benchmark Books, 1997.

Lightfoot-Klein, Hanny. *Prisoners of Ritual: An Odyssey into Female Genital Circumcision in Africa*. Binghamton, N.Y.: Harrington Park, 1989.

Metz, Helen Chapin, ed. *Sudan: A Country Study*. Washington, D.C.: Library of Congress, 1992.

Peterson, Scott. *Me Against My Brother: At War in Somalia, Sudan, and Rwanda*. New York: Routledge, 2000.

Petterson, Donald. *Inside Sudan: Political Islam, Conflict, and Catastrophe*. Boulder, Colo.: Westview Press, 1999.

Spaulding, Jay, and Stephanie Beswick. *White Nile, Black Blood: War, Leadership, and Ethnicity From Khartoum to Kampala*. Lawrenceville, N.J.: The Red Sea Press, 2000.

Walgren, Judy. *The Lost Boys of Natinga: A School for Southern Sudan's Young Refugees*. Boston: Houghton Mifflin, 1998.

INTERNET RESOURCES

http://www.sudanembassyus.org

The official web site of Sudan's embassy in Washington offers news and press releases from the government's viewpoint as well as information about Sudan's economy, tourism, government, and people.

http://www.sudan.net

Information about Sudan's weather, society, education, and culture, Sudanese music downloads, and news about the country from Reuters, the BBC, and other media organizations.

http://www.nubasurvival.com

Explores the culture of the Nubas from their music and poetry to their customs and celebrations.

http://www.stockton.edu/~gilmorew/consorti/1iafric.htm

Information about the ancient history of Sudan, including photos of a royal tomb at Meroe, an example of Meroitic script, and maps of ancient Cush.

http://www.sudmer.com

Sudan's foreign ministry web site gives news about the country and statistics.

http://www.sufo.demon.co.uk/cons002.htm

The text of Sudan's 1998 constitution.

INDEX

Numbers in **bold italic** refer to captions.

INDEX

PICTURE CREDITS

CONTRIBUTORS

The FOREIGN POLICY RESEARCH INSTITUTE (FPRI) served as editorial consultants for the MODERN MIDDLE EAST NATIONS series. FPRI is one of the nation's oldest "think tanks." The Institute's Middle East Program focuses on Gulf security, monitors the Arab-Israeli peace process, and sponsors an annual conference for teachers on the Middle East, plus periodic briefings on key developments in the region.

Among the FPRI's trustees is a former Secretary of State and a former Secretary of the Navy (and among the FPRI's former trustees and interns, two current Undersecretaries of Defense), not to mention two university presidents emeritus, a foundation president, and several active or retired corporate CEOs.

The scholars of FPRI include a former aide to three U.S. Secretaries of State, a Pulitzer Prize–winning historian, a former president of Swarthmore College and a Bancroft Prize–winning historian, and two former staff members of the National Security Council. And the FPRI counts among its extended network of scholars—especially its Inter-University Study Groups—representatives of diverse disciplines, including political science, history, economics, law, management, religion, sociology, and psychology.

DR. HARVEY SICHERMAN is president and director of the Foreign Policy Research Institute in Philadelphia, Pennsylvania. He has extensive experience in writing, research, and analysis of U.S. foreign and national security policy, both in government and out. He served as Special Assistant to Secretary of State Alexander M. Haig Jr. and as a member of the Policy Planning Staff of Secretary of State James A. Baker III. Dr. Sicherman was also a consultant to Secretary of the Navy John F. Lehman Jr. (1982–1987) and Secretary of State George Shultz (1988).

A graduate of the University of Scranton (B.S., History, 1966), Dr. Sicherman earned his Ph.D. at the University of Pennsylvania (Political Science, 1971), where he received a Salvatori Fellowship. He is author or editor of numerous books and articles, including *America the Vulnerable: Our Military Problems and How to Fix Them* (FPRI, 2002) and *Palestinian Autonomy, Self-Government and Peace* (Westview Press, 1993). He edits *Peacefacts*, an FPRI bulletin that monitors the Arab-Israeli peace process.

GAIL SNYDER is a freelance writer who holds a degree in journalism from Pennsylvania State University. She has also written a book for young readers on George Washington's childhood. Gail lives in Chalfont, Pennsylvania, with her husband, Hal Marcovitz, and children, Michelle and Ashley.